NEEDLEPOINT *for* CHAIRS, SEATS & STOOLS

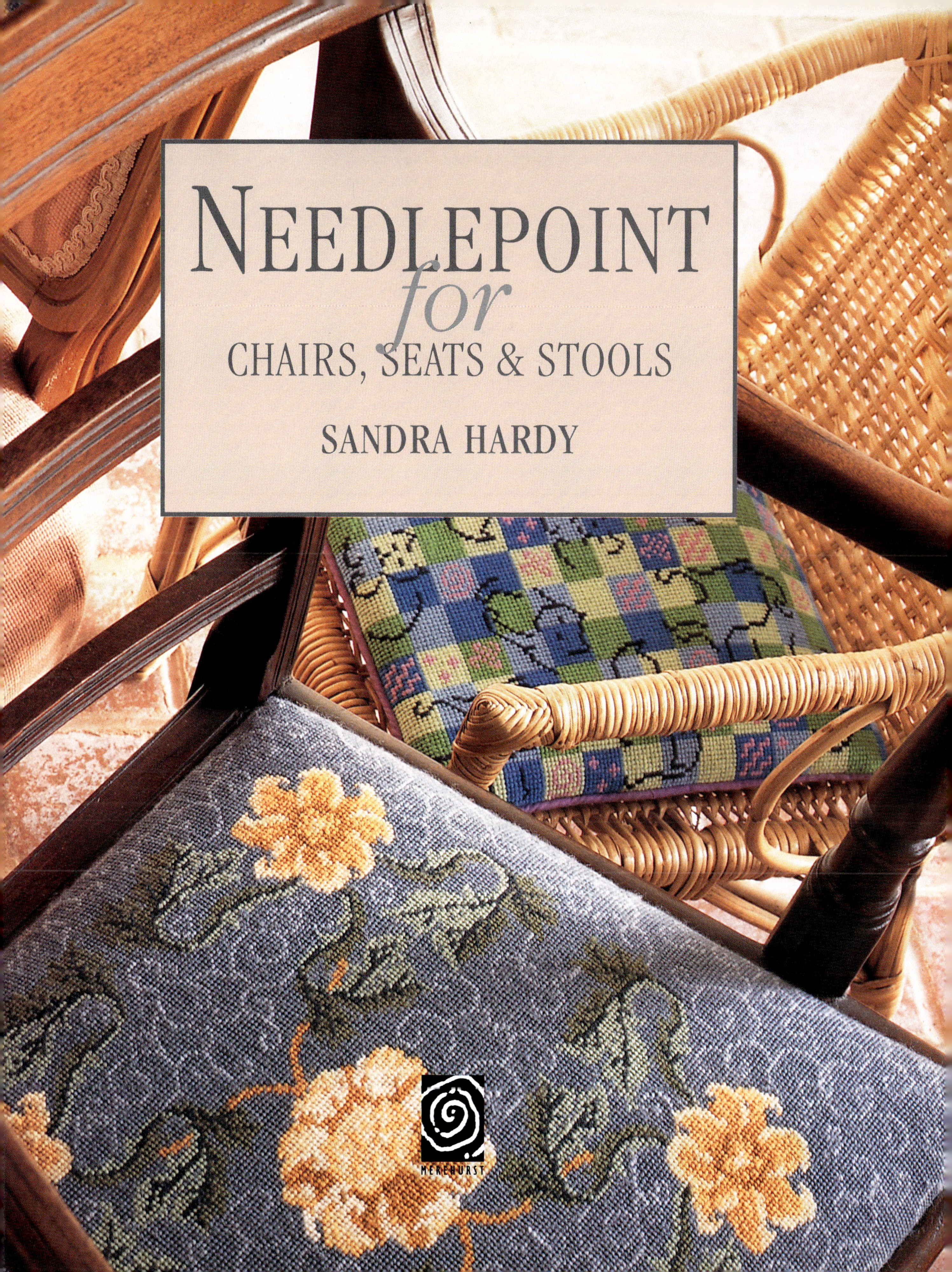

NEEDLEPOINT *for* CHAIRS, SEATS & STOOLS

SANDRA HARDY

MEREHURST

Introduction

This book joins together the ancient craft of needlepoint with the more recent skills of upholstery. It is an ideal combination utilising the hardwearing and durable nature of needlepoint as a covering fabric, while providing perfect surfaces for displaying the wonderful stitching. In the past there have been many periods when needlepoint was unrivalled as an upholstery fabric, even from the earliest rudimentary attempts at stuffing and padding a chair seat. Today the widespread enthusiasm for all needlecrafts has again led to a keen interest in using needlepoint in this way.

The projects include a wide variety of designs, from the traditional Victorian lilies and William Morris style flowers, to the very modern patterned fish and chequered cats. Designs are symmetrical, random, bordered, repeat patterned, realistic, imaginary, exciting and relaxing. Yarns are varied as are the canvas sizes and types, employing many different stitches. All basic information for these needlepoint elements together with a wealth of hints, tips and suggestions for successful stitching can be found in the needlepoint requirements section.

The furniture used for the projects again varies enormously from real antiques to junk shop finds. The ages of these range from the 150-year-old prayer chair to a 1995 reproduction stool. They include between them all the main types of upholstered seats, from the simplest drop-in construction, progressing to the 'pin-cushion', 'top-stuffed' and sprung seat. There are both traditional and modern versions wherever appropriate, which differ in the materials, techniques and tools required. Each project has a cross section diagram clearly showing the layers involved in the construction. A list of likely faults and problems together with appropriate remedies is also included to help you decide on the action to be taken with your particular chair. Instructions for all the techniques, together with information on materials and tools are given in the section on upholstery requirements.

An important section in each chapter contains suggestions for varying the design and adapting it to fit any size and shape of seat. This versatility also means that a much-liked design can be used for a completely different age and style of chair. In this way it is hoped that everyone's taste in furniture can be accommodated.

First published 1995 by Merehurst Limited,
Ferry House, 51-57 Lacy Road, London SW15 1PR

Created, edited and produced by Rosemary Wilkinson Publishing,
4 Lonsdale Square, London N1 1EN

ISBN 1-85391-424-X

A catalogue record for this book is available from the British Library.

The right of Sandra Hardy to be identified as the Author of this Work has been asserted by her in accordance with the Copyright, Designs and Patents Act 1988.

Designed by Bill Mason
Photographs by Marie-Louise Avery
Illustrations by Kate Simunek
Charts by Jonathan Harley

Colour separation: Columbia Offset, Singapore
Printed in Hong Kong by Midas

Contents

William Morris Chair

Drop-in seat; traditional

Drop-in seats, sometimes known as loose seats or trapseats, are removable from the chair or stool frame. They were first seen in large numbers during the Queen Anne period at the beginning of the 18th century and, by the end of the century, had become a firm favourite nationwide. The great Georgian designers, Chippendale, Sheraton, and Hepplewhite, found the simple drop-in seat the ideal partner for their beautifully carved chair backs. During the Regency period, the drop-in seat was adapted to suit the classical chair styles, but then disappeared completely in the Victorian era with the advent of springs. It was not until the Arts and Crafts movement, early in the twentieth century that the drop-in seat re-emerged to satisfy the demand for simpler styles. These seats provided an excellent base for the highly patterned William Morris fabrics and swirling Art Nouveau designs.

The chair in this project is probably late Regency, but without the typical sabre legs. William Morris's Kennet design, printed in 1883 and featuring curvaceous flowers and leaves, is the inspiration for the needlepoint.

To stitch the design

Finished size: depth, 51cm (20in)
back width, 38cm (15in)
front width, 46cm (18in)

MATERIALS

Materials are given for the size of chair above. To measure up for your own chair, see pages 98 and 109.

Canvas: 12hpi, mono de luxe, white, size 63 x 58cm (25 x 23in)

Thread: Anchor tapestry wool in the following shades:

8006, 8062	*1 skein each*
8052, 8058,	
8060, 8838	*2 skeins each*
9002, 9020	*3 skeins each*
8832	*5 skeins*
8834	*24 skeins*

Needle: tapestry size 18

Stitches: continental tent throughout; using one strand of tapestry wool

INSTRUCTIONS

Follow the chart on pages 8, 9, 12 and 13. Mark the centre of the canvas and use to position the middle flower. Complete all the flowers and leaves, then go on to the swirls in the background. Finally, stitch the actual background using shade number 8834, starting from the top and working downwards.

To adapt the design

This chair seat is actually a very large size drop-in and it is likely that many others will be of smaller dimensions, especially across the front. Often in sets of dining chairs, the carvers will have larger dimensions than the others.

• The background area around the main pattern can be reduced if the measurements required are slightly smaller. If a much larger reduction in size is necessary, the four outer side leaves could be omitted, leaving the width of the main pattern only 32cm (12⅝in). This, with the addition of varying amounts of background, would fit virtually all drop-in seats (fig. 1).

1

• Similarly, if the depth from back to front is too large, the four centre leaves at top and bottom of the design could be omitted (fig. 2).

2

• Many of the modern drop-in chairs today have much squarer seats, rather than tapering towards the back. A suitable design could be achieved by making up a block pattern, using either of the two flowers shown in fig. 3 and fig. 4.

3

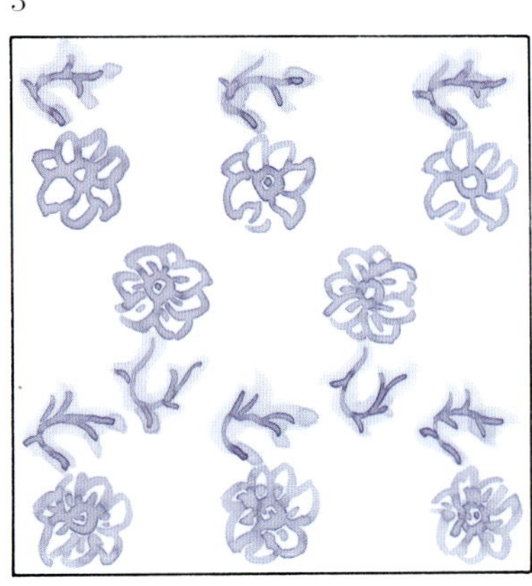

• The background pattern is made up of randomly placed small swirls, which can be easily added or removed as the main pattern is altered.

• The colours of the yarns selected for this design resemble the original Kennet ones quite closely. However, many people have interior colour schemes on the opposite half of the colour wheel, that is in greens and pinks. A small sample has been stitched to illustrate the effect that this would create (see page 11).

Anchor tapestry wools in these shades have been used:

9022
9002
8904
8786
8344
8346
8352
8402
8006
9252

4

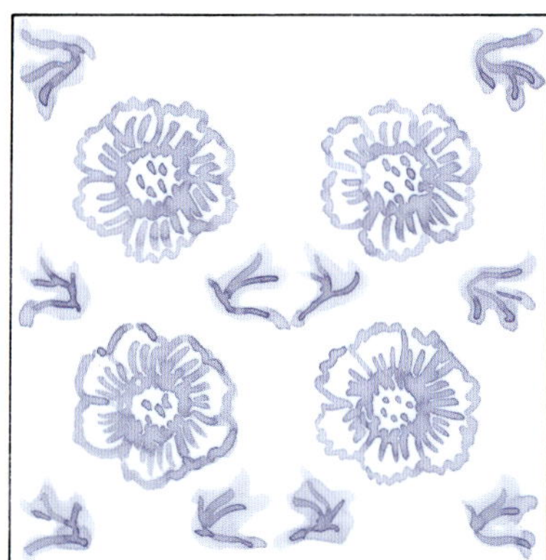

To upholster a drop-in seat using traditional methods and materials

The seat should have a firm, slightly rounded shape, sloping gently from the centre to the sides. The layers in the seat should be as shown (fig. 5). If the underneath of the seat is not in a good state of repair when the old top covering fabric is removed, likely problems are :

Fault	*Remedy*
Broken or sagging webbing	The webbing must be replaced, or tightened up if it is still relatively new and in good condition. In each case, all the existing upholstery will need to be removed.
Hollow or lumpy seat	When the webbing is repaired, the hollowness of the seat may also be rectified. If not, then the stuffing will need to be cleaned and re-teased, or replaced, depending on what it is made of.
Calico cover omitted, so padding and stuffing visible	Carefully attach the new calico without agitating the existing layers. Linterfelt is notoriously difficult to re-arrange smoothly once disturbed.

A common problem with drop-in seat style chairs is that the joints often become split and loose because the seat itself, covered in a very thick material, or even several layers of top covering fabric, is forced into the frame. The frame must be repaired by replacing broken dowels if necessary, or by glueing then clamping. The seat frame itself will probably need to be shaved a little at the sides to make it smaller, so that the same problems do not recur.

5

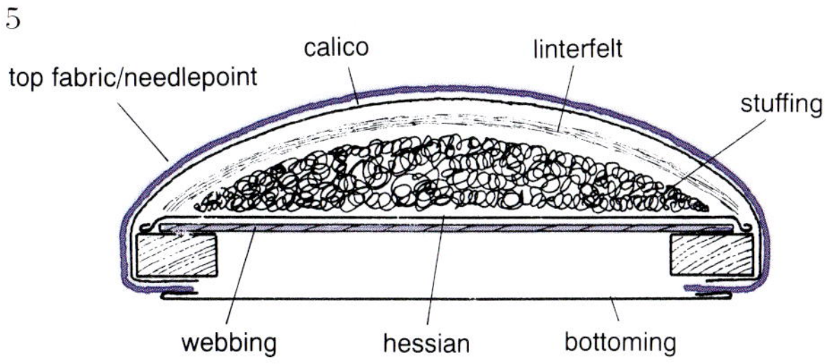

MATERIALS (for complete re-upholstering)

Black and white webbing: 2.5m (8ft 3in)
12oz hessian: 55 x 62cm (21⅝ x 24⅜in)
Mattress twine: 2.5m (8ft 3in)
Stuffing: 0.5kg (1lb)
Linterfelt: 50 x 55cm (19¾ x 21¾in)
Calico: 56 x 66cm (22 x 26in)
Tacks: 250gm of 13mm (½in) improved, and 10mm (⅜in) fine
Bottoming (black): 40 x 51cm (15¾ x 20in)

A stitched sample of the alternative colourway

METHOD

1 Attach the webbing and hessian on the top side of the frame.

2 Make the bridle loops, each with about 2.5cm (1in) slack, measuring over your fingers laid flat on the hessian.

3 Arrange the stuffing so that it is fairly tightly packed with slightly more in the centre, and sloping downwards towards the outside edges.

4 Place over the linterfelt, so that none of it extends over the side edges of the seat frame. Watch that it does not creep down while the calico is pulled over tightly. If any linterfelt is left covering the seat frame it will make it too bulky to fit into the chair frame.

5 Attach the calico and needlepoint to the underside of the seat frame, with the corners pleated as necessary. Tack the bottoming in place.

VARIATIONS

1 If the seat frame is a convex curve from side to side, then care must be taken for all the layers to follow this shape. When attaching the webbing

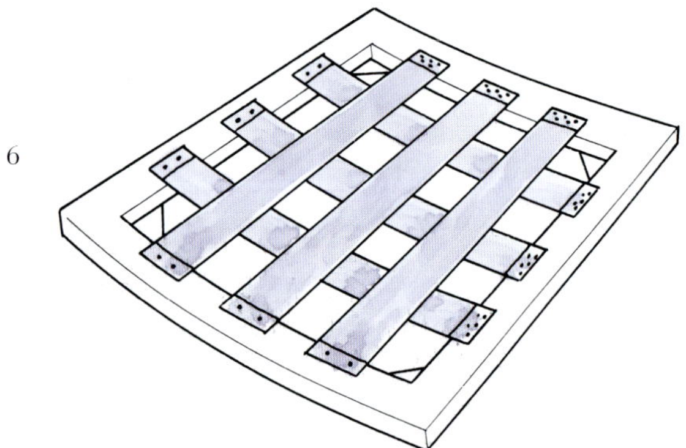

6

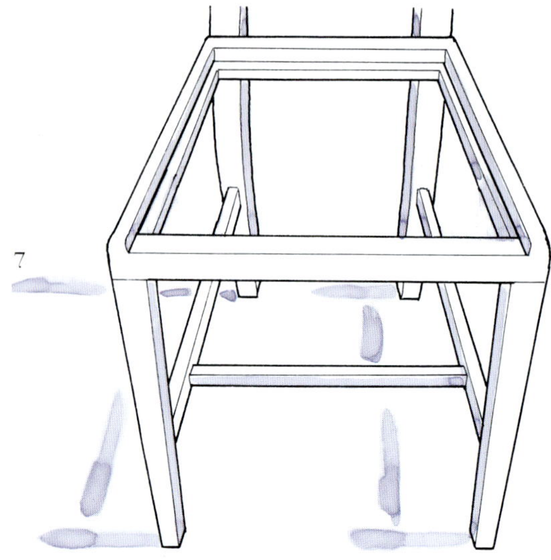

7

sideways, webs are not interwoven but laid underneath the back-to-front strips (fig. 6).

2 Regency style drop-in seats fit between the side rails of the chair frame, and are prevented from slipping down by dowels, screws or corner supports (fig. 7). Cut the hessian about 15cm (6in) longer and attach, leaving the extra at the front. Make a firm roll of stuffing, usually about 2-2.5cm (1in) thick, tucking the hessian under the stuffing, and securing with tacks (fig 8). The rest of the seat is upholstered in the normal way as described above.

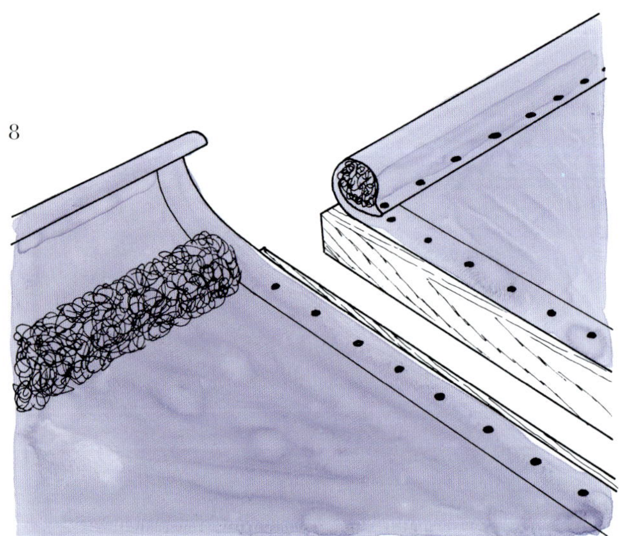

8

Tropical Fish Chair

Pin-cushion seat; modern

To stitch the design

Finished size: depth, 32cm (12½in)
back width, 27cm (10½in)
front width, 34cm (13½in)

MATERIALS

Materials are given for the size of chair above. To measure up for your own chair, see pages 98 and 109.

Canvas: 14hpi, mono deluxe, antique, size 46 x 48cm (18 x 19in)

Thread: Appletons tapestry wool in the following shades:

431, 462, 471, 884	*1 skein each*
101, 472, 473, 524, 525, 526, 759, 944, 945	*1 hank each*
105, 465, 821, 823	*2 hanks each*

Needle: tapestry size 20

Stitches: continental tent for the main design and borders; basketweave for the background; using one strand of tapestry wool throughout

Pin-cushion or pin-stuffed upholstery is always very flat or shallow, and is most commonly found on post-Victorian furniture in the early part of this century. By then chair frames had not only become simpler in style but also lighter in weight, even spindly, to such an extent that many have not survived to the present day. The chair used for this project was originally caned but, like so many others, became damaged and was eventually discarded.

The cane holes in the frame have been filled with a mixture of very fine sawdust and wood glue. Once set, this produces a strong surface for tacking or stapling into. The seat is upholstered in modern materials, which are fixed more easily into the narrow tacking space with staples than with tacks. Staples also inflict less strain on the chair frame. It is for this reason that many pin-cushion seats, as well as valuable antique chairs, are repaired or re-upholstered with staples.

The frame has been painted, rubbed down with a fine steel wool, then finished with gold wax to create a sparkly effect and an attractive, up-to-date piece of furniture.

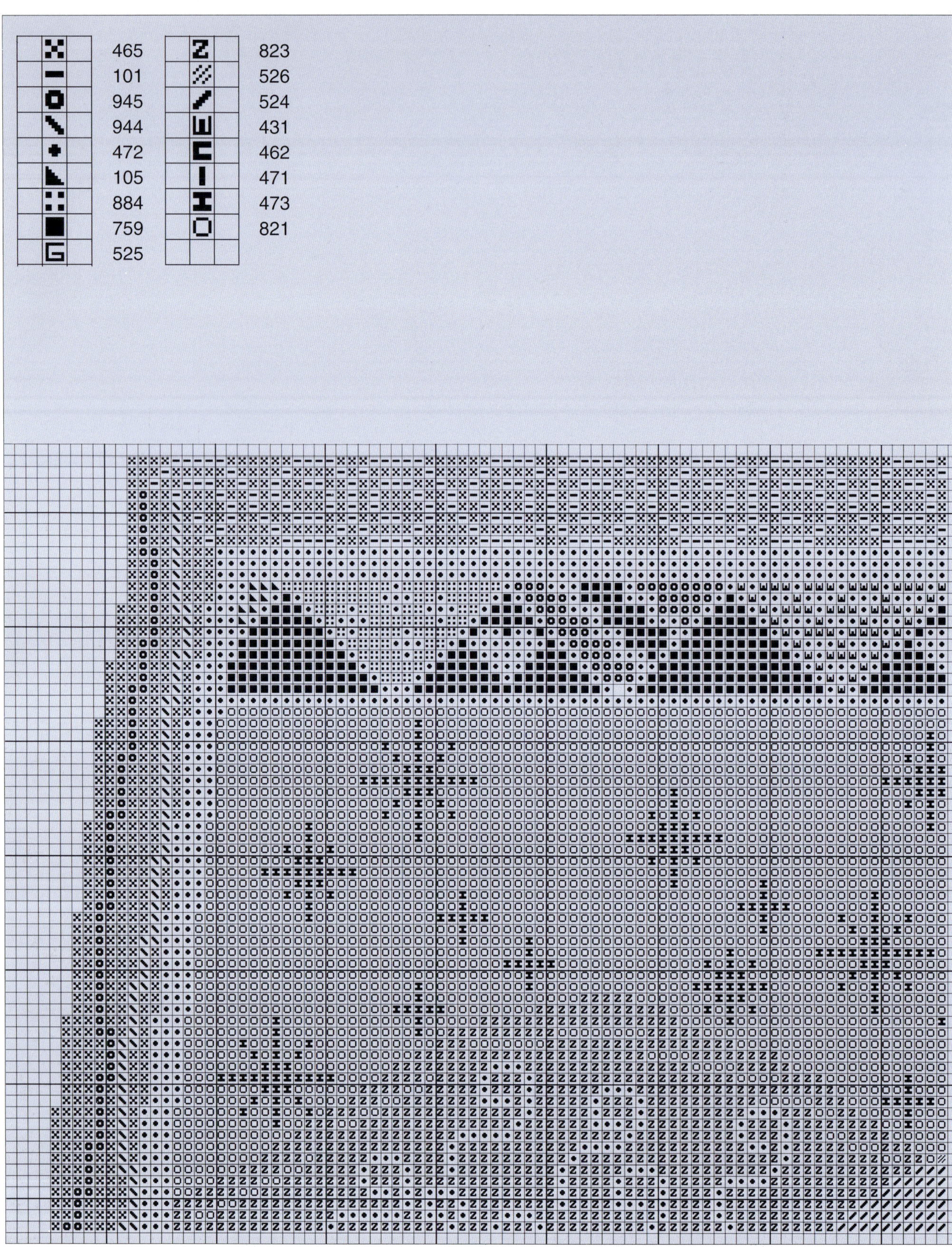
465
101
945
944
472
105
884
759
525
823
526
524
431
462
471
473
821

Tropical Fish Chair

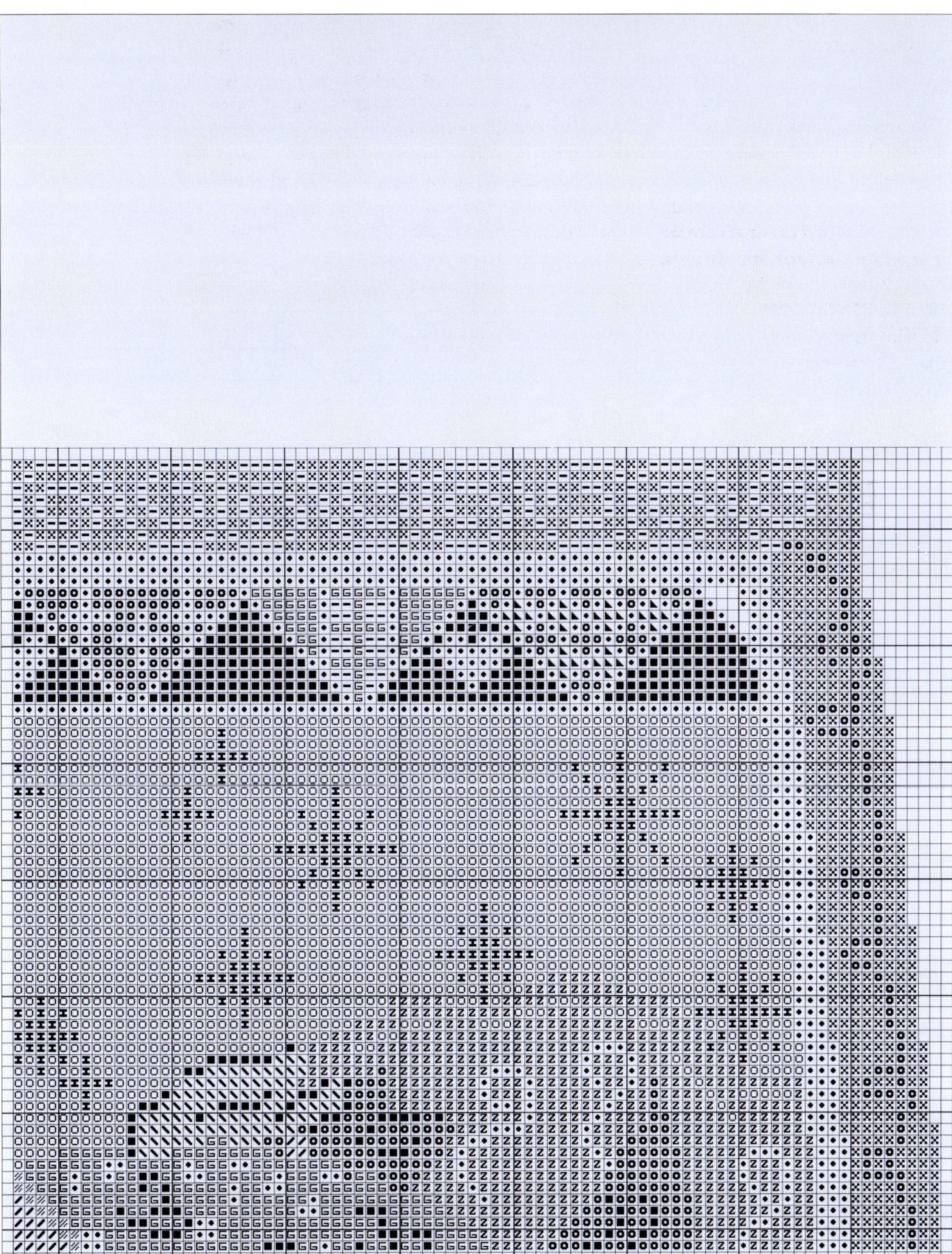

continued on page 20

To adapt the design

The random background pattern and optional border make this design highly adaptable.

• Use a different count of canvas. For a larger seat, 12hpi will give you 39 x 37cm (15⅜ x 14⅝in) instead of 34.5 x 32cm (13½ x 12½in); while 10hpi will give you 47 x 45cm (18½ x 17¾in). For a smaller seat, 16hpi will give you 29 x 28cm (11½ x 11in). In this case, you will need to use two strands of crewel wool instead of one strand of tapestry wool.

• Add in more borders around the edges, or remove them. The outer borders measure 2cm (¾in) in width, the inside ones 13mm (½in). Suggestions are illustrated on page 22 and charted below.

• For a square seat, simply extend the side border areas to fit. All the background motifs are randomly positioned, so it is quite easy to add one or two more to fill the extra space required (fig. 1).

1

• If your chair is completely different - for example, a drop-in or a sprung seat - a plain background could be added to fit all sizes. In this case, the patterned design becomes a central motif (fig. 2).

2

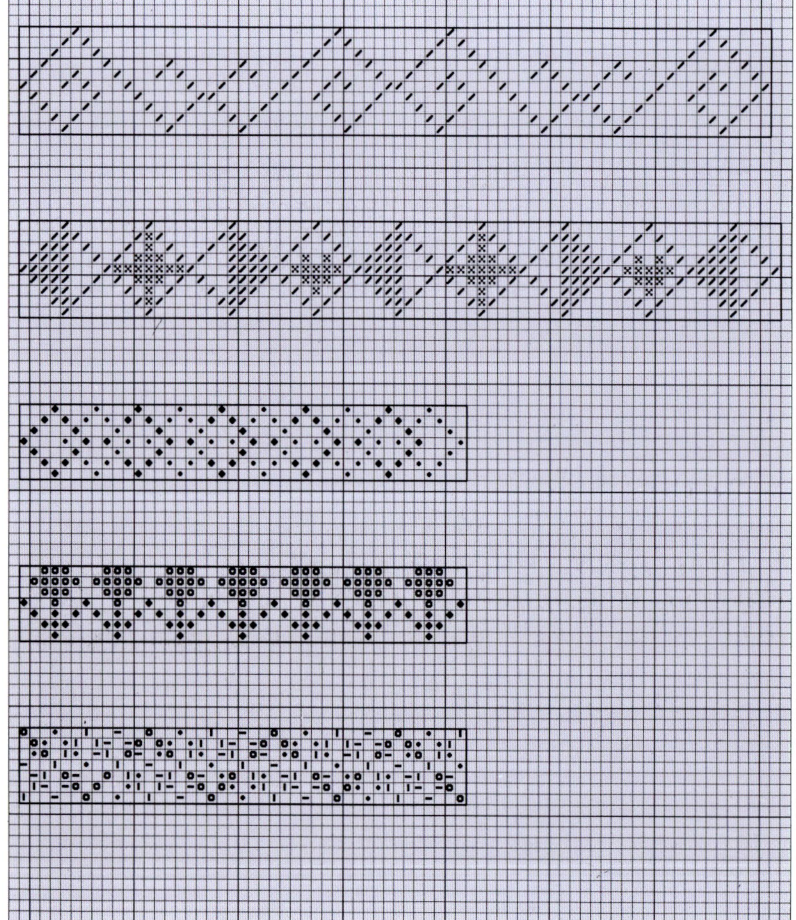

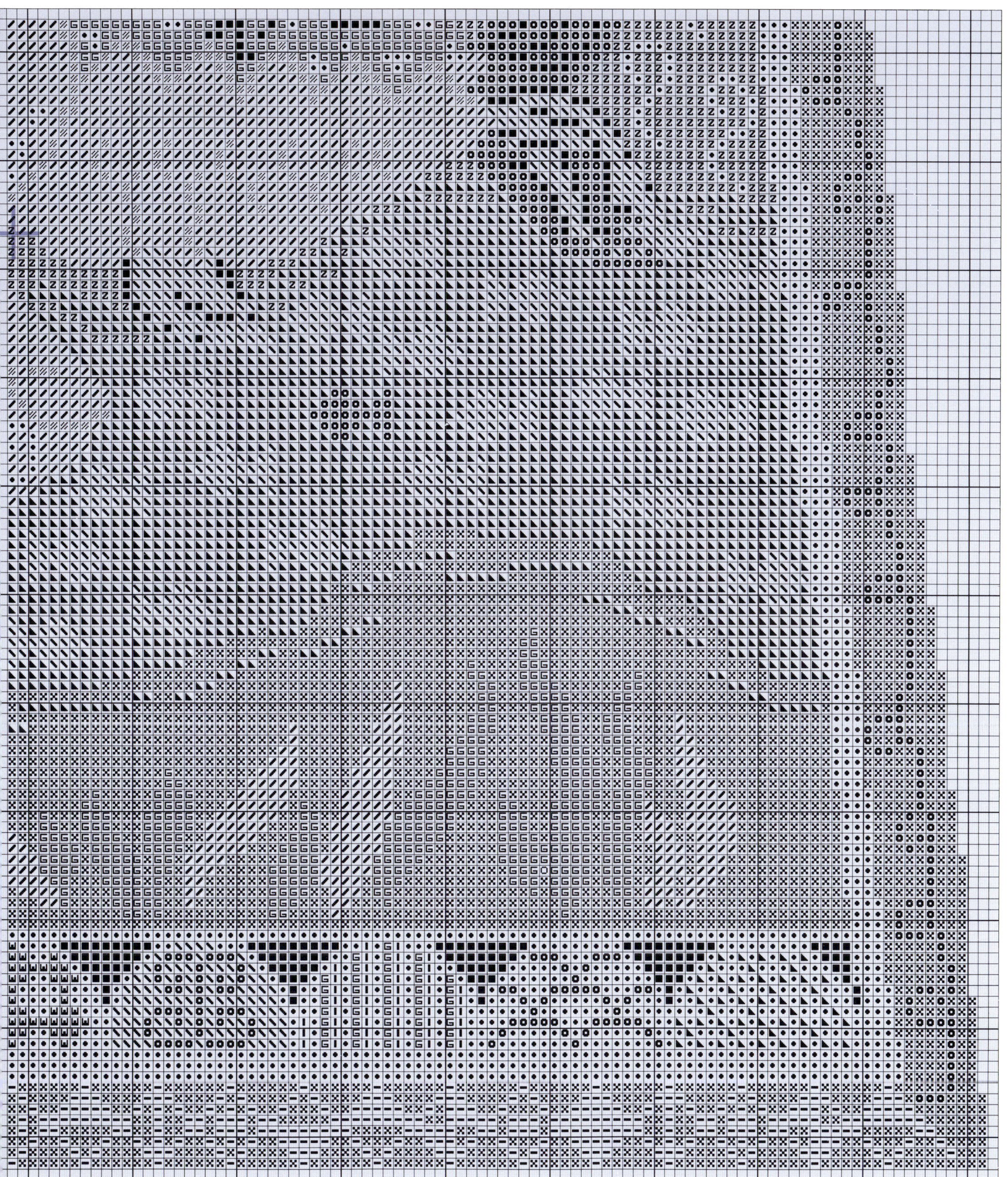

INSTRUCTIONS

Follow the chart on pages 16, 17, 20 and 21. Mark the centre vertical and horizontal lines on the canvas to use as reference points when positioning the fish and patterns. Count the threads and mark the top and bottom borders. Start stitching the patterns on the large fish, then fill in the whole shape of fish. Next stitch the small fish, curls, stars, and water weeds, moving on to the border lines. Fill in the borders and, finally, stitch the background colours.

Stitched samples of additional border designs

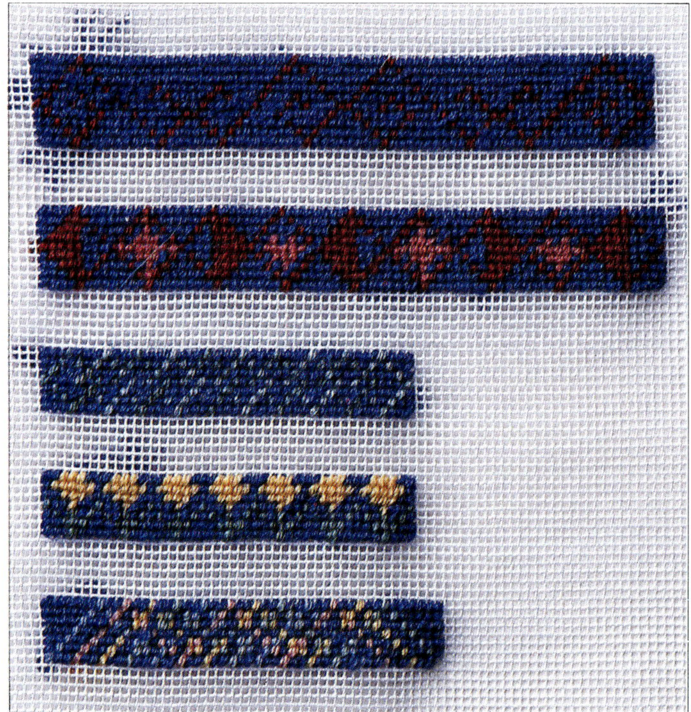

3

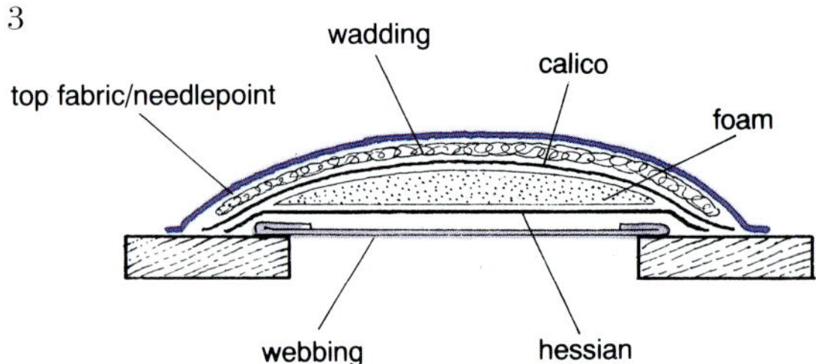

To upholster a pin-cushion seat using foam

The seat should be very slightly padded, with sides gently sloping to the show-wood frame. The layers should lie as in fig. 3. If the seat looks the right shape, and feels smooth and even, simply attach the needlepoint. If not, then use the following chart to help identify the problems and how to rectify them.

Fault	*Remedy*
Broken, sagged webbing or ripped hessian	Replace.
Flat or uneven seat	Replace any old foam or padding with a new piece of polyurethane foam.

MATERIALS (for complete re-upholstering)

Black and white webbing: 1.5m (5ft)
12oz hessian: 42 x 40cm (16½ x 15¾in)
Flame retardant foam: seating quality, size 31 x 33cm (12¼ x 13in)
Calico: size 38 x 40cm(15 x 15¾in)
2oz polyester wadding: 32 x 34cm (12⅝ x 13⅜in)
Staples: size 10 and 13mm (⅜ and ½in)
Plaited braid (see method): strands of tapestry wool each approximately one and a half times the outside measurement of the cushion

METHOD

1 If the chair frame has not been upholstered before, draw a line onto the frame to mark which part will be tacked into and which will remain as show-wood.

2 Interweave and attach two strips of webbing in both directions to the top of the frame, using five 13mm (½in) staples instead of tacks.

3 Attach the hessian in the usual way, using 10mm (⅜in) staples.

4 Place over the foam, having turned in the edges so that it sits fractionally inside the drawn lines.

5 Place over the calico and staple with smaller staples. Start in the centre of each side and move out to the corners. Apply an even 'pull' on the calico, so the foam creates a smooth curved edge.

6 Trim the calico close to the staples and place over the wadding, then attach the needlepoint by folding under the unstitched edge and stapling.

7 Make the plaited braid by alternating the two steps: left thread over one thread; right thread over, under and over (fig. 4). Attach the braid over the canvas edges, either by slip stitching or by using clear adhesive. Make the join at the centre back and butt up the ends. If these appear bulky, a small clamp can be placed on top until they flatten.

4

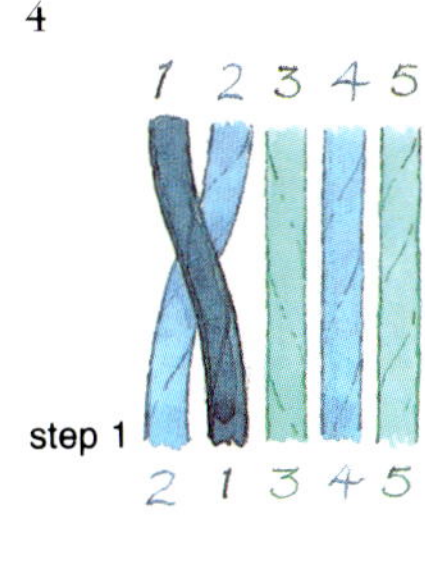

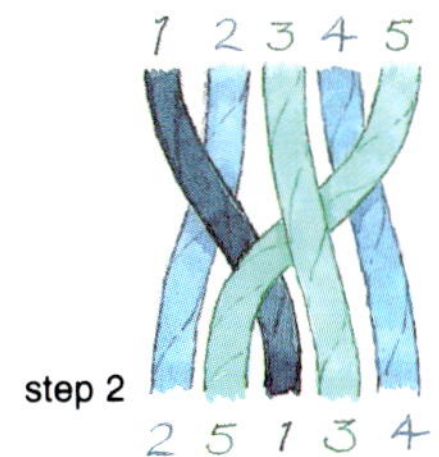

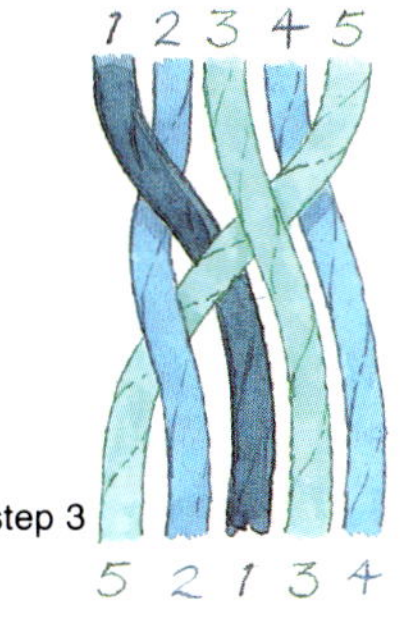

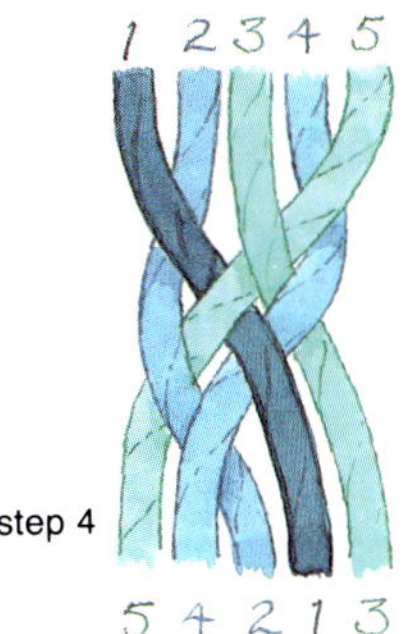

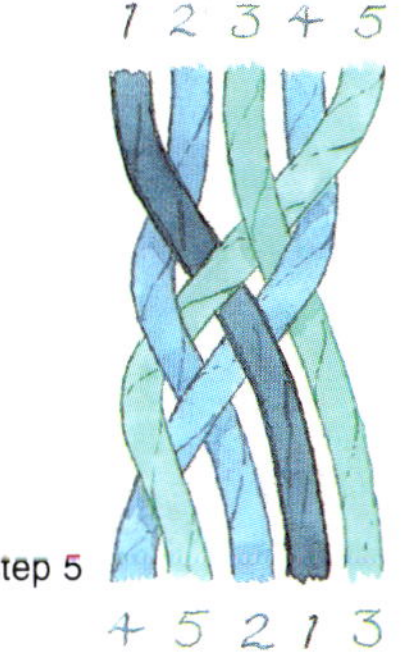

To adapt the design

Drop-in seats, as seen in the first project, do vary considerably in size, not only in the overall dimensions but in the actual shape of the seat. Sides can be very angled or form a complete square, as for many stools. This needlepoint design of horizontal rows of patterns is therefore more than suitable for making these adjustments.

• If the seat is wider, or the angles of the sides different, the rows of patterns are easily extended or reduced. Remember, however, to match up the centre of the patterns with the centre of the canvas, ensuring that the overall needlepoint design will remain symmetrical.

• Additional rows of patterns are illustrated below left if the length of the needlepoint needs extending (charted in fig. 3, page 28). The colours are the same as the chart on page 29 plus navy. The same pattern may be added to the front as well as the back, or you can use a different one, depending on personal preference. These new rows can be either placed beyond the existing rows or inserted between them. Remember to allow the two rows of background stitching between any additional rows, in order to retain the overall uniformity of the design.

• If this design is to be used for a much larger item, for example, a long stool, and a coarser texture more similar to a rug or carpet is required, then use a 8hpi canvas stitched with double tapestry wool. The existing design would be increased in depth from 42cm (16½in) to 51cm (20in). Adjustments can then be made by removing or adding on rows of patterns as necessary.

• Colour changes can be made easily by substituting one or more shades of wool. An interesting version would be to reverse the colour at a random point along each row as shown in the photograph below right.

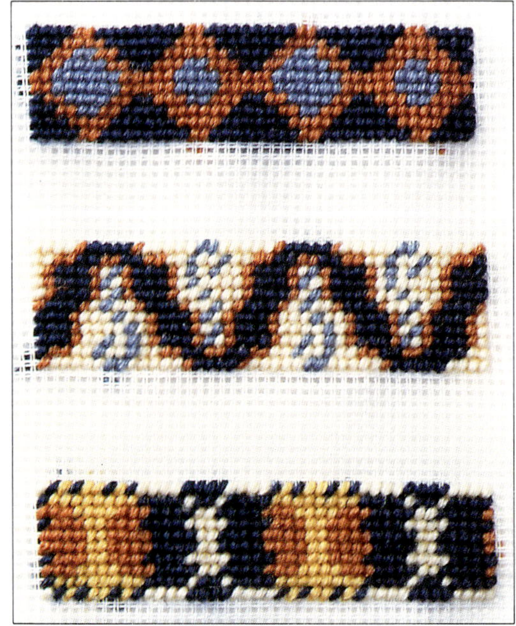

METHOD

1 Attach the webbing, if needed, and hessian on the top side of the frame.

2 Trim the rubberised hair piece, so that it is 0.5cm (¼in) larger on all sides than the seat size and place over the hessian.

3 Lay over the linterfelt, removing any excess so that its edges are level with the frame edges.

4 Attach the calico to the underside of the frame, then lay over the polyester wadding. Tack the needlepoint to the underside of the frame, then cover over with bottoming to complete.

4

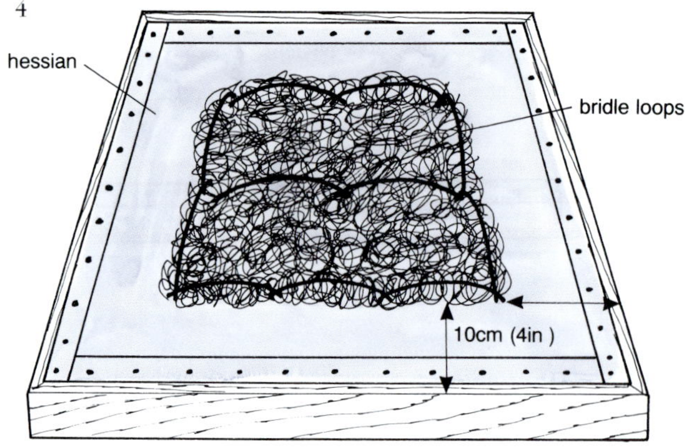

5

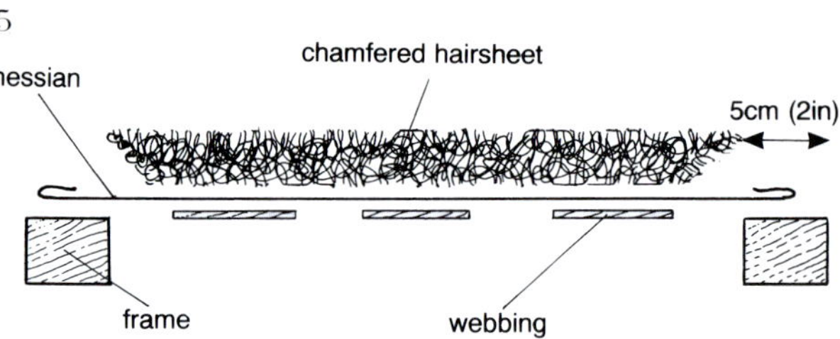

3

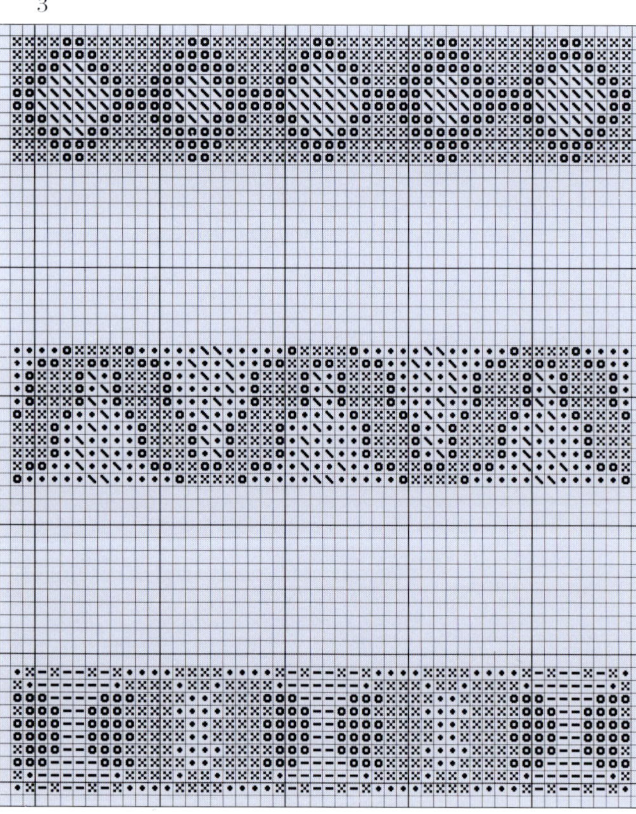

VARIATIONS

This method gives a flat-shaped seat; if a more domed effect is preferred, there are two alternative methods:

1 Insert several flat bridle loops on the hessian extending to within 10cm (4in) of the frame (fig. 4). Insert a thin layer of teased, loose fibre or hair, then cover over with the rubberised hair sheet.

2 Cut another piece of rubberised hair about 5cm (2in) smaller than the frame on all sides, and cut the larger piece an extra 1cm (⅜in). Chamfer the edges of the smaller piece and lay in the centre of the hessian (fig. 5). Cover with the larger piece of hair sheet and continue as before.

Chart of additional pattern rows

7176
7593
7472
7579
7297
reverse design

A close-up detail of the Kilim design

Louis XV-Style Dining Chair

Top-stuffed seat; panel back; traditional

To stitch the design

Finished size:

Seat:	depth, 58.5cm (23in) back width, 53.5cm (21in) front width, 68.5cm (27in)
Rear back: Panel:	depth, 37cm (14½in) minimum width, 32cm (12⅝in) maximum width, 38cm (15in)
Front back:	depth, 38cm (15in) minimum width, 33cm (13in) maximum width, 39cm (15⅜in)

MATERIALS

Materials are given for the size of chair above. To measure up for your own chair, see page 33.

Canvas: 12hpi mono de luxe, white in the following sizes: 71 x 81cm (28 x 32in); 48 x 48cm (19 x 19in); 49 x 49cm (19¼ x 19¼in)

Thread: Anchor tapestry wool in the following shades:

8792	*3 skeins*
8294	*4 skeins*
8330	*5 skeins*
8786	*7 skeins*
8788	*10 skeins*
9442	*16 skeins (3 hanks)*
8326, 8322	*55 skeins each*

Needle: tapestry size 18

Stitches: continental tent throughout; using one strand of tapestry wool

The chair used in this project is a reproduction of a typical Louis XV style, with its curved sides and cabriole legs. During Louis XV's reign in the 18th century, France dominated chair design and upholstery techniques, influencing not only Britain but all of Europe. Upholstery methods had been considerably improved and refined, so that precise curved and straight edges could be produced by careful stuffing and stitching. Prior to this, stuffings were simply mounded in the centre of a seat and held in place by nailed top covers.

Panel back chairs, such as this one, used to be placed in a strict formal layout of long lines against the walls. The chair back was therefore never decorated and fabric panels were usually only of a plain linen or cotton, while the front covering was of sumptuous silk, velvet, tapestry or brocade. This, however, had changed entirely by the early 1800s, when chairs were given permanent positions in the centre of a room. This project has needlepoint panels on front and back.

INSTRUCTIONS

Mark the centre of the canvas for both the seat and front back panels to position the first diamond. The chart on pages 36 to 37 shows just over half of the arrangement of diamonds for the seat. Start with the centre diamond in the top row (righthand diamond on page 36). For the back there are ten diamonds in four rows of two, three, two and three. The centre point falls between two diamonds, so start with the one on the left. Stitch all the diamond outlines before working on the flower motifs. Next, fill in the beige background areas (shade number 9442). Finally stitch the stripes, starting at the centre top of one of the diamonds and working upwards. For the outer back panel, fold the canvas in half widthways to find the centre vertical line as a position guide for the middle stripe on the chart on page 38. The needlepoint will need to be blocked back to shape.

Fault	*Remedy*
SEAT	
Hollow and depressed	This is very likely to happen as, without springs, there is only the density of stuffing to retain the shape. Even when the stuffing is very tightly packed and of good quality, some compression will eventually occur with use. Remove the covers down to the uppermost layer of stuffing and, if it is hair, re-tease, adding more to achieve a better shape. If, however, the webbing has sagged, this will contribute to the hollow shape. The only method of repair is to remove it and start from scratch.
The sides are overhanging the frame	This sometimes occurs when the stitched edges have been poorly made, with large gaps left between the rows allowing the hessian to bulge out. Insufficient stuffing and poor regulating can also contribute to the problem. Alternatively, if the stitched edges are in good condition, then a series of tucks or pleats can

BACK

If the outside back fabric is attached to the chair before the front, then all the padding and layers must be removed in order to position it. On some chairs, usually Edwardian ones, however, the outside back panel is actually tacked onto the outside of the frame and the raw edges and tacks are covered with braid. On these, repairs can be made to the inside padding and layers as necessary.

Fault	*Remedy*
Feels lumpy with more stuffing in the lower part	Remove any layers so that the stuffing is visible. It is likely that this has slipped down over time; the bridle loops may have disintegrated or were perhaps omitted. Re-stitch new bridle loops in vertical lines and re-stuff. This problem occurs with all vertically stuffed areas, as can be seen later in the padded box project.
The outer back has bulged to an unsightly shape, probably leaving the front panel hollow	Webbing strips are often omitted on these back panels because of the narrow width of the tacking rails. This puts greater strain on the hessian which, with time, will 'give' and even disintegrate, allowing the stuffing to escape. Remove all the layers as necessary and replace.

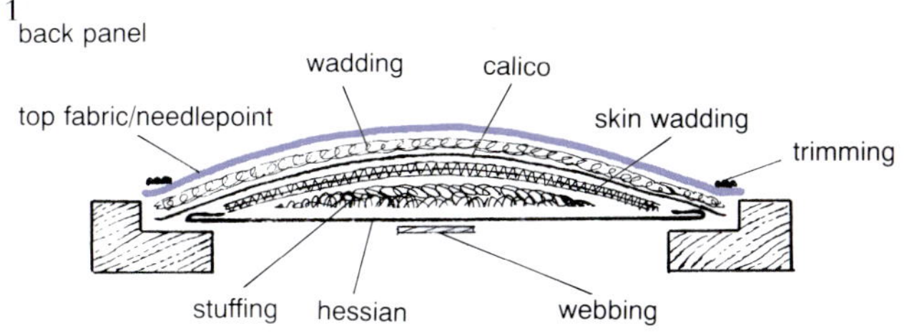

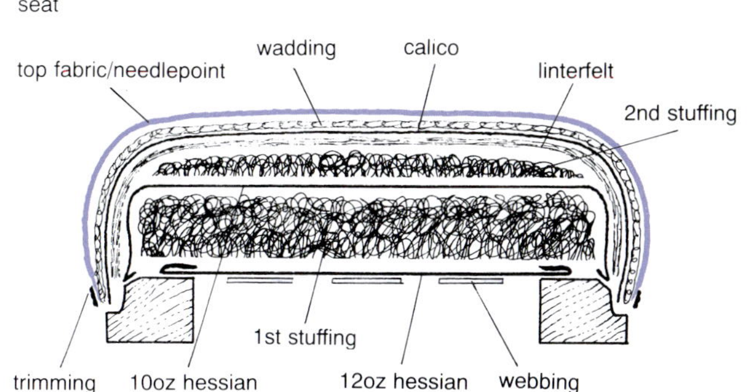

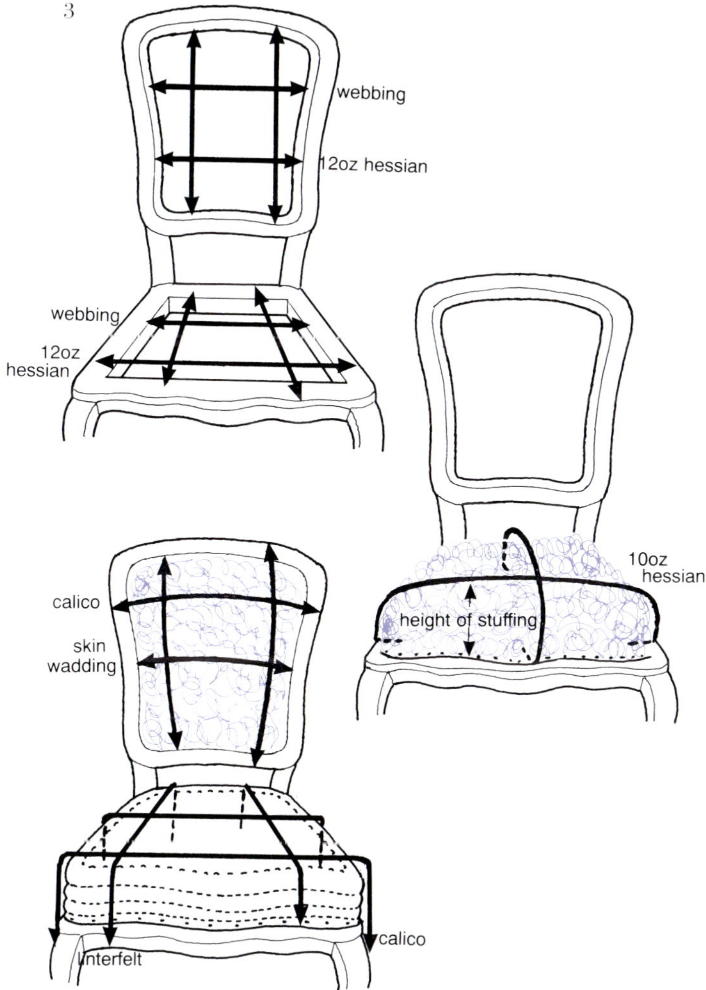

To upholster a top-stuffed chair with a back panel using traditional methods

The seat should be slightly domed in the centre, with vertical sides down to the frame. The back panel should be firm to touch, yet slightly convex, following the curve of the frame. The layers should be as shown in fig. 1 and fig. 2.

The convex nature of this panel means that all layers need to be tacked first down the length, then around to the sides, in order to retain the curve. Any widthways webbing strips will be placed behind the vertical ones rather than interwoven, in a similar way to the convex drop-in seat as shown on page 14.

Possible problems with this style of chair are shown in the chart opposite.

MATERIALS (for complete re-upholstering)

Black and white webbing
12oz hessian*
Mattress twine: 3.5m (12ft)
Stuffing: 1.5kg (3lb)
10oz hessian*
Linterfelt*
Calico*
2oz (50g) polyester wadding*
Tacks: 13mm (½in) improved and 10mm (⅜in) fine
Coloured gimp pins
Adhesive: colourless fabric adhesive
Braid/gimp: 3.2m (11ft)
Skin wadding*
Mattress needle

*As each chair frame is likely to vary slightly in dimensions from the one used here, I have shown where to measure for each layer of material, rather than give exact quantities (fig. 3). Add 2 cm (¾in) turnings on all sides for the webbing, hessian and calico and note that the linterfelt is taken to the tacks on the seat frame and the skin wadding for the back panel is measured over the stuffing. For the needlepoint measure as follows, adding 5cm (2in) unstitched canvas on all sides to each piece.
seat and front back panel: over wadding to edge of show-wood;
outer back panel: to edge of show-wood

To adapt the design

The needlepoint design is based on the carved flower motif on the actual chair and simply repeated within a diamond grid. The gently undulating stripes surrounding the diamonds reflect the curved frame.

• The striped background makes it easier to adapt the design to different sizes and shapes of chairs. The layout of the diamonds on the back panel reflects the line of the wooden frame, but this can be altered to suit many other shapes: for example, oval, shieldback, arched and oblong (fig. 4). If preferred, the diamond grid can extend to the edges of the needlepoint, replacing all the striped background areas.

• For a less formal effect, the diamond grid can be replaced by background; this would leave a regular, half-drop pattern. However, the stripes must be left in their existing positions or removed completely. They cannot be increased to touch the flowers as there is insufficient contrast in colour.

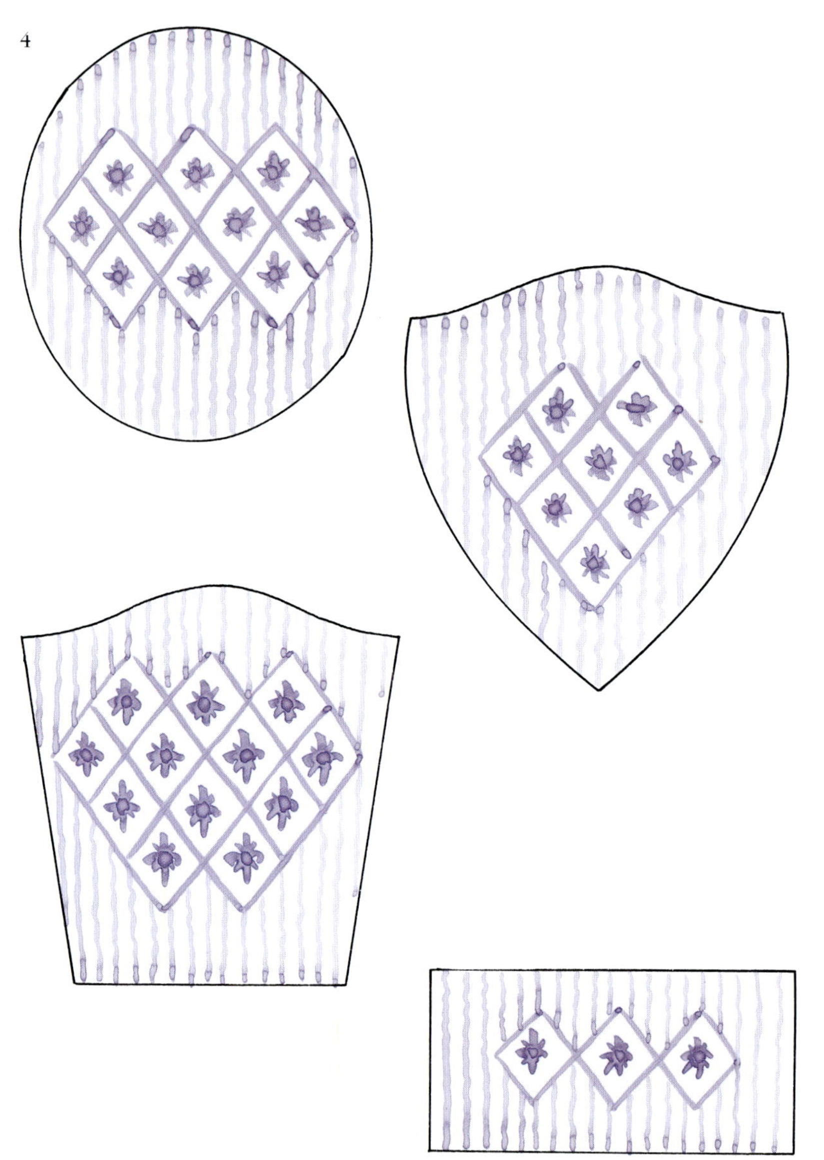
4

METHOD Seat:

1 Interweave five strips of webbing from back to front, with four strips sideways to top of frame.

2 Attach 12oz hessian and stitch bridle loops, allowing two fingers upright slack on each.

3 Place the stuffing under the loops, packing it in tightly and evenly. Add extra stuffing around the edges so that the sides are vertical with the frame.

4 Cover with 10oz hessian, stitch the stuffing ties and tack the folded hessian onto the chamfered

8330
8786
8792
8788
8294
8322
8326
9442

continue design

edges. Take care that this follows the curved shape of the frame at the front.

5 Stitch two rows of blind stitching and a roll edge, then attach a small amount of stuffing under flat bridle loops.

6 Cover over with linterfelt and attach the calico to the sides of the frame. Cut round the back struts (fig. 5). Place the corner fold so that it is actually touching the strut, without any wrinkles of fabric underneath. Cut to within 1cm (⅜in) of this fold, at a 90° angle to it.

5

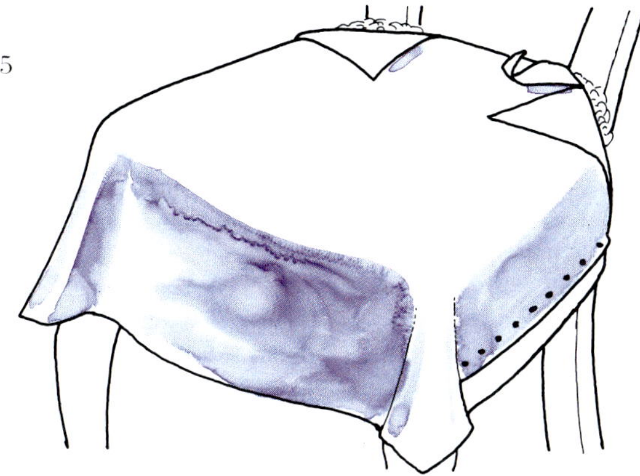

7 Place over polyester wadding and, finally, the needlepoint cover, making sure that the centre diamonds are positioned correctly.

8 Cover the folded canvas edges with a braid or gimp trimming. A gimp is the more suitable of the two as it stretches around curves, rather than puckering. Alternatively, use a plaited trimming, as described on page 23.

METHOD Back:

1 First attach the outer back panel of the needlepoint onto the front side of the frame, checking from the back that the stripes are vertical before hammering the tacks home.

2 Place one webbing strip lengthways and one widthways, covering over with 12oz hessian.

3 Proceed as for the Musical Cherubs Piano Stool on page 54 stitching vertical bridle loops and maintaining the curved shape of the back as far as possible. Finish with a matching trim.

A view of the needlepoint on the outer back panel

Decorative Stitch Display Stool

Sprung stool; traditional

Stools have featured in domestic seating since the earliest times and, up until the beginning of the 17th century, predominated over chairs. Throughout the Georgian period in the 18th and early 19th centuries, stools were often included in a drawing room to add variety to the sets of identical chairs; these had both drop-in and fully upholstered seats, made in the current styles of the day. Stools were still plentiful in the Regency era, but were used for more specific purposes - such as for a piano or a dressing table - rather than for everyday seating. Victorian times saw every shape and style of stool, including the popular, round adjustable-height piano stool.

Up until 1830, all these stools consisted of stuffing and stitching, but were non-sprung. Although coil springs had been used earlier in coaches, carriages and for exercise horses, it took several years for upholsterers to adapt them successfully for seating, improving both comfort and design potential.

This stool features a needlepoint top worked in an eye-catching display of decorative stitches with colour-matched velvet sides.

To stitch the design

Finished size: 55 x 40cm (21½ x 16in)

MATERIALS

Canvas: 15hpi single de luxe, antique, size 65 x 50cm (26 x 21in)
Thread: 2ply variable dyed wool Colinette yarn
in dark blue, green and purple 1 hank
DMC Broder Médicis
8996, 8208 *2 skeins each*
Needle: tapestry size 20
Stitches: blocks of Byzantine, diagonal Scotch, cushion and reversed cushion, vertical and horizontal satin, Florentine and Hungarian diamond; using one strand of main wool, with an additional strand of crewel wool where necessary on long straight stitches.

INSTRUCTIONS

Follow the plan on page 44 for the placement of the various blocks of stitches. In between the blocks and for the frame round the centre rectangle, work a diagonal stitch over two threads. Using the photograph as a rough guide, cut the various colours from the hank as required. However, it is unlikely that your hank will match this one exactly, so some of the colours here may change slightly.
Mark the border position on the canvas and start stitching from the top working downwards to avoid rubbing the yarn. Follow the diagrams for the individual stitches given on pages 92 to 94.

To adapt the design

This design includes several decorative stitches which date back to the origins of canvas-work itself. They are given an up-to-date look through the use of variable dyed wool.

• Numerous alternative decorative stitches can be used. However, experiment first to test canvas coverage and comparative density to others selected. Also bear in mind that stitches over 1cm (⅜in) long will become easily snagged and do not provide the required hardwearing surface. Suitable stitches are: diagonal mosaic, Milanese and triangle, see pages 93 and 94.

• The arrangement of the blocks of stitches can have any number of variations. This versatility makes the project suitable for any other size or shape required.

To upholster a traditionally sprung stool

(Frame size: 55 x 40cm (21½ x16in)
The stool top must be very slightly domed in the centre, but generally level all over. The sides should be vertical and, when sat upon, the seat should feel comfortable with no lumps or hard areas. The layers in the stool are as shown in fig. 1. If the stool is quite old, it is likely that several problems may exist with the upholstery.

1

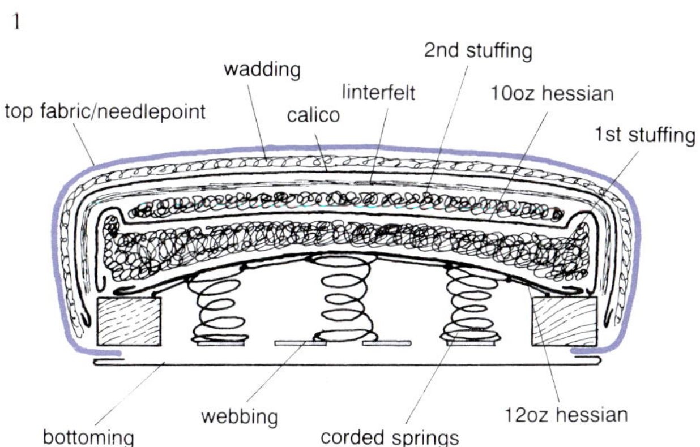

Fault	*Remedy*
Webbing sagged or broken	Replace.
Broken, buckled, distorted or rusty springs	As a general rule, springs should be replaced if they have been used for a number of years. However, if in doubt, test each spring by pressing up and down to see if it still depresses vertically as it should, not at a distorted angle. Also, if it compresses easily to its base, its resilience is weakened and it must be replaced.
Worn hessian either over the springs or on the stitched edges	Replace the hessian as its strength has deteriorated.
When sat upon the seat feels hollow	The stuffing is now overly compressed; if the surrounding upholstery is in good condition, simply add extra stuffing and a new piece of linterfelt, as this also compresses substantially with time.

MATERIALS (for complete re-upholstering)

Black and white webbing: 2.6m (8ft 7in)
Springs: 6 x 4in, 9½ gauge
Laid cord: 6.5m (21ft 3in)
12oz hessian size: 65 x 50cm (25¼ x 19¾in)
Mattress twine: 10m (11yds)
Horsehair/fibre: 1.5kg (3lb)
10oz hessian: 75 x 60cm (29½ x 23⅝in)
Linterfelt: 70 x 65cm (27½ x 25½in)
Calico: 80 x 65cm (31½ x 25⅝in)
2oz polyester wadding: 80 x 65cm (31½ x 25⅝in)
Tacks: 16mm (⅝in) improved, 13mm (½in) improved and 10mm (⅜in) fine
Matching colour fabric: 2 pieces, 43 x 16cm (17 x 6¼in); 2 pieces, 59 x 16cm (23¼ x 6¼in)
Matching colour cord: 2m (2¼ yds)
Small curved needle
Matching thread
Mattress needle
Bottoming: 56 x 41cm (22 x 16½in)

METHOD

1 Attach six strips of webbing to underside of frame from front to back in three pairs; and three strips interwoven from side to side (fig. 2).

2 Secure the six springs in two rows of three and lace down, covering over with 12oz hessian.

3 Stitch the bridle loops using two fingers upright and stuff before attaching the 10oz hessian on the chamfered edges and stitching the stuffing ties.

2

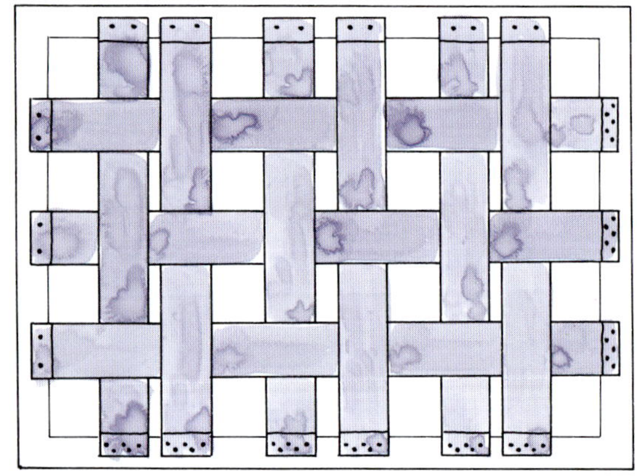

4 Two rows of blind stitching and a roll edge will give firm sides to the stool.

5 Add a thin second stuffing, then linterfelt and calico. Finally lay over the wadding to finish the upholstery, ready for the needlepoint.

6 Join the four strips of fabric by machine sewing making 1.5cm (½in) seam allowances from the edges. Join this band to the stitched canvas placing

3

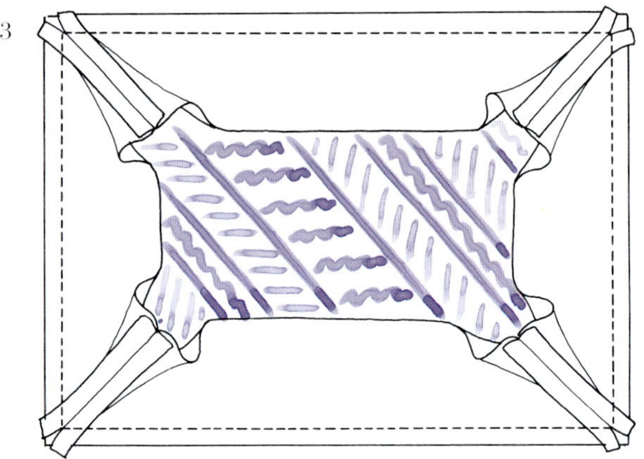

4

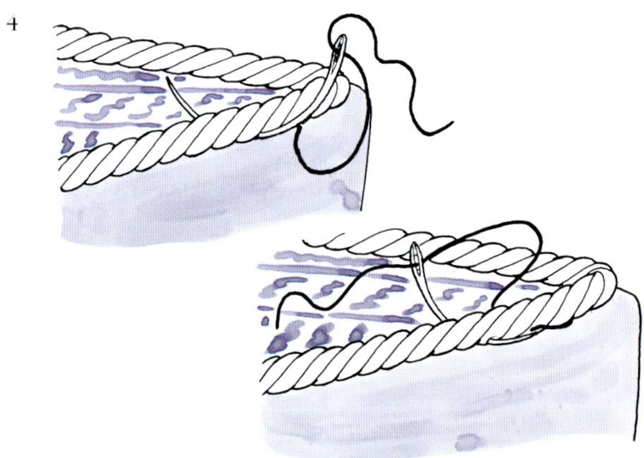

right sides together. The corners of the band will need to be snipped in order to fit smoothly (fig. 3). Place over the calico and tack the raw edges to the underside of the stool. Stitch the cord trimming over the needlepoint and fabric seam using a small curved needle and strong thread (fig. 4). Bottoming covering the underneath completes this project.
If your stool has a show-wood then the needlepoint must be folded and tacked up to it, and the edges covered with a decorative trimming.

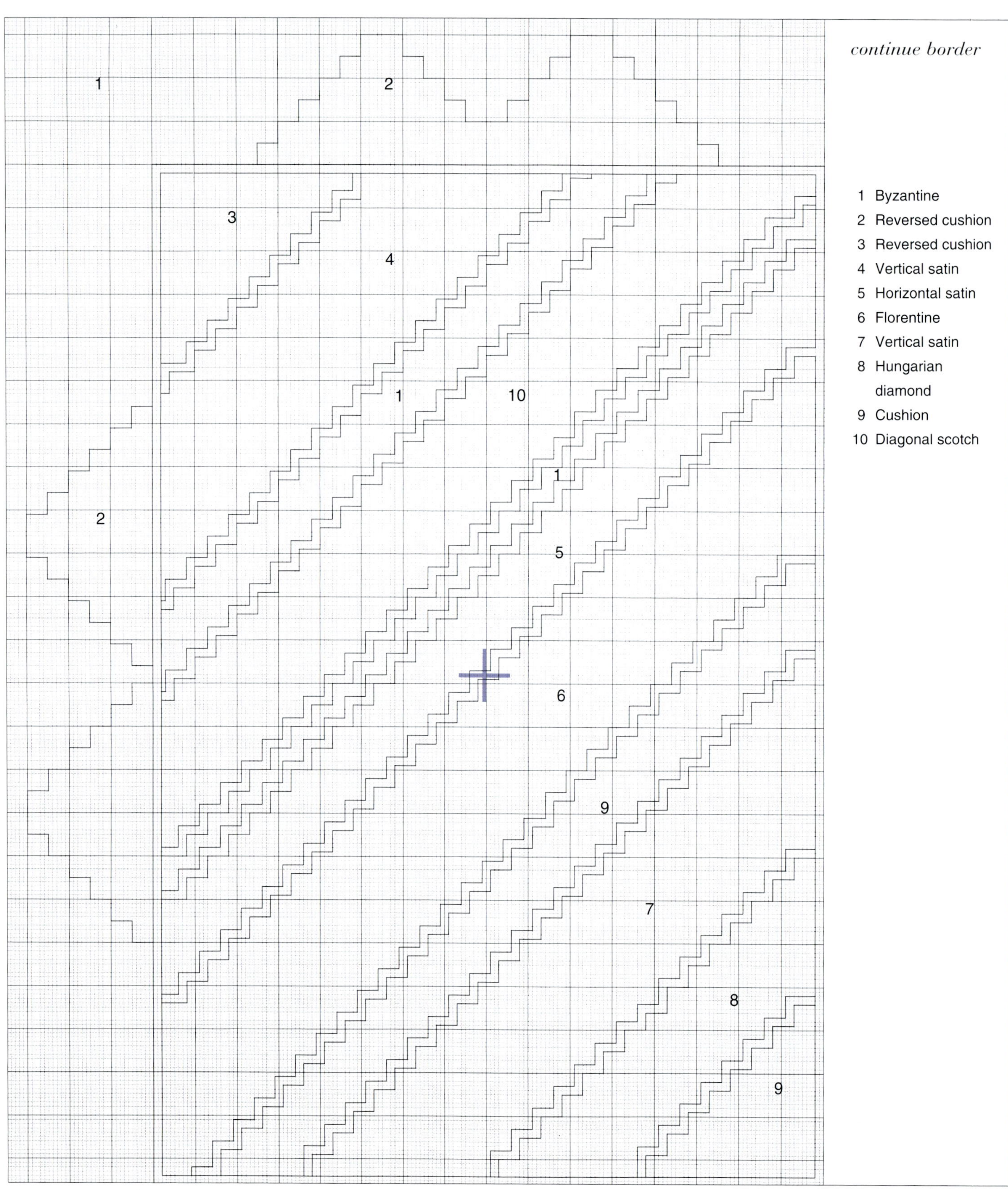

1 Byzantine
2 Reversed cushion
3 Reversed cushion
4 Vertical satin
5 Horizontal satin
6 Florentine
7 Vertical satin
8 Hungarian diamond
9 Cushion
10 Diagonal scotch

Wild Poppies Footstool

Drop-in footstool; modern

To stitch the design

Finished size: 33cm (13in) diameter circle

MATERIALS

Materials are given for the size of footstool above. To measure up for your own footstool, follow the instructions for the drop-in seat on page 98.

Canvas: 12hpi mono de luxe, antique, size 42.5cm (17in) square

Thread: DMC Broder Médicis crewel wool in the following shades:

8100, 8104, 8106,	
8107, 8110, 8111,	
8113, 8119, 8122,	
8123, 8126, 8127,	
8164, 8166, 8173,	
8176, 8341, 8401,	
8402, 8410, 8411,	
8417, 8419, 8420, 8506	*1 skein each*
8128, 8129, 8139,	
8168, 8175	*2 skeins each*
8314, 8328	*9 skeins each*

Needle: tapestry size 18

Stitches: continental tent for the flowers and leaves; Byzantine for the background; using four stands of crewel wool throughout

Footstools were very much a Victorian item of furniture. Prior to this time, stools were taller and larger, and were used primarily for seating. However, in Victorian interiors, it was considered almost a necessity to have a footstool for each chair. These were often produced to match the shape and design of the chair legs, a trend left over from late 17th century interiors where stools were actually made as part of a suite of chairs and tables. The Victorians also liked to fill all available floor space with small pieces of furniture - for example, screens, stands, tables and, of course, stools.

A great variety of styles, materials and decorative finishes were used. Some footstools were even made into 'spittoons', with hinged lids revealing metal or china containers. Of course, all these footstools provided an ideal medium for the much-loved Berlin woolwork, often with beadwork embellishments, of which numerous charted patterns were readily available. In recent years with the resurgence of interest in embroidery, many reproduction footstools have become available, ideal for displaying needlepoint.

To adapt the design

This needlepoint design was inspired by my local countryside, where wild poppies spring up indiscriminately among the corn and wheat fields. Mixed shades of crewel wool create the detailed shading of colour and depth in the poppies. Continental tent stitch is the ideal stitch for working the numerous small areas of colour, whereas the background employs the attractive Byzantine stitch (see page 94). This creates a contrast to the smaller tent stitch, as well as speedily covering the canvas. The slight mottled effect of the background, achieved by mixing colour strands, has provided additional interest.

• The design can be easily adapted for oval, square or hexagonal shaped stools of a similar size by adding varying amounts of background. For slightly smaller sizes, change to a 14hpi canvas; the design will then become a 30.5cm (12in) diameter circle.

• For a more formal effect, a diamond, square, hexagonal or other geometric shaped grid can be drawn around one of the poppies, then repeated over the area (fig. 1 and fig. 2). Alternatively, an oblong design, extending from the back to the front of the stool, can made (fig. 3). All these variations can be stitched for much larger stools.

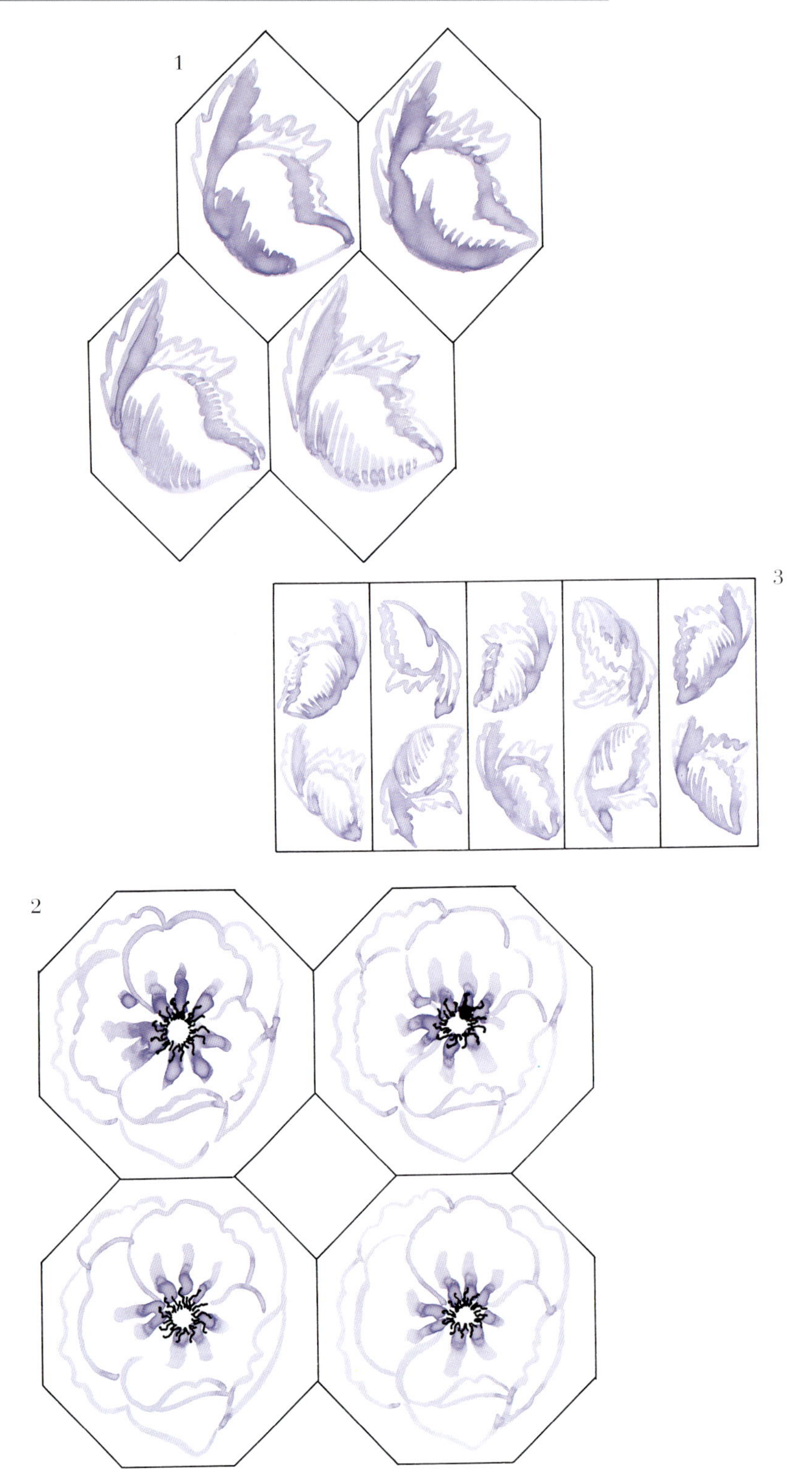

Wild Poppies Footstool

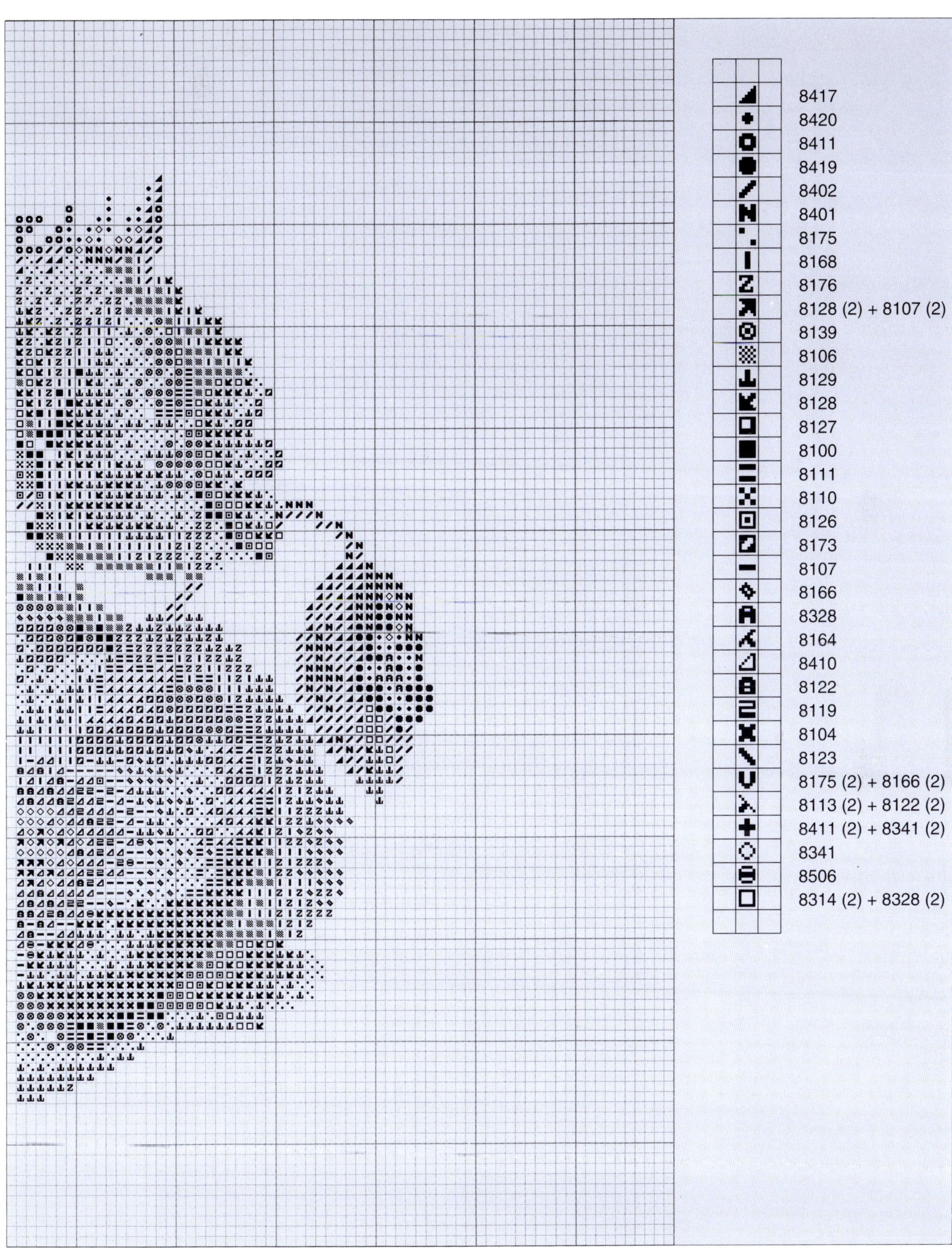

INSTRUCTIONS

Follow the chart on pages 48 and 49. Draw a circle from the centre of the canvas with a radius of 16.5cm (6½in). Mark the centre of the canvas and use this, with the chart centre, to position the two poppy centres. Complete these, then the petals, followed by the leaves. As the colour combinations in the needle are constantly changing, use several needles to save on re-threading time. Stitch the background starting at the top of the marked circle and working downwards, using two strands of 8314 mixed with two strands of 8328. Take care to match up the Byzantine pattern when the two sides rejoin underneath the poppies. Half-size stitches will have to be made to fill in round the poppies and leaves.

Fault	*Remedy*
Padding exposed as the calico layer is missing	If the padding is still in a satisfactory shape and has not broken up into pieces, then simply cover with a new layer of calico. However, if further investigation reveals very flat, dirty and dusty stuffing and wadding, remove and completely re-upholster (refer to the traditional drop-in seat instructions on page 11).
The padding/ stuffing looks too flat	Remove the layer of linterfelt or wadding and add a small amount of stuffing to the existing quantity, securing this under any bridle loops if possible. Place over a new piece of linterfelt and cover with calico.

To upholster a modern foam-filled footstool

This stool should have a dome-shaped pad which is firm but springy, and evenly sloping on all sides. The layers should be as drawn in fig. 4.

4

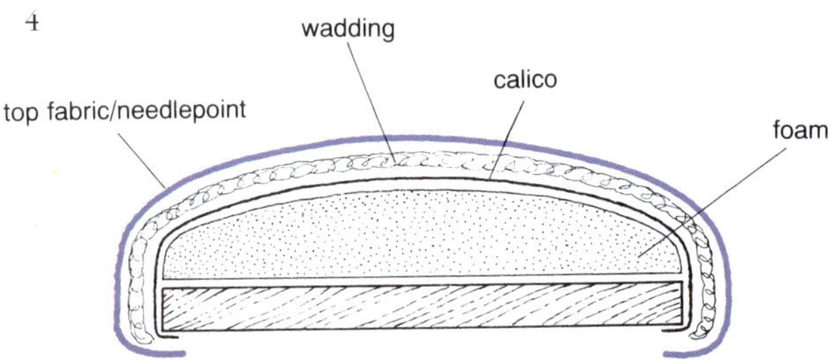

If your stool is a foam-padded one used over several years, it is best to substitute a new piece of combustion modified foam of seating quality. A new piece of calico is preferable to re-using calico that has probably become worn.

If the stool is an older one, probably Victorian, when the covering fabric is removed, then a number of problems could be present as detailed above.

MATERIALS (for complete re-upholstering)

Wooden base: 26cm (10¼in) diameter
Combustion modified polyurethane foam: 5cm (2in) thickness, seating density, 28cm (11in) diameter
Glue: rubber-based or spray glue for foam upholstery
Calico: 41cm (16⅛in) square
Staple gun and staples: 10mm (⅜in) staples (if not available use a hammer and 10mm (⅜in) tacks)
2oz polyester wadding: 28cm (11in) diameter circle

METHOD

1 Chamfer the underside of the foam (fig. 5). Dab a small amount of glue onto the chipboard base and place the foam centrally over this.

5

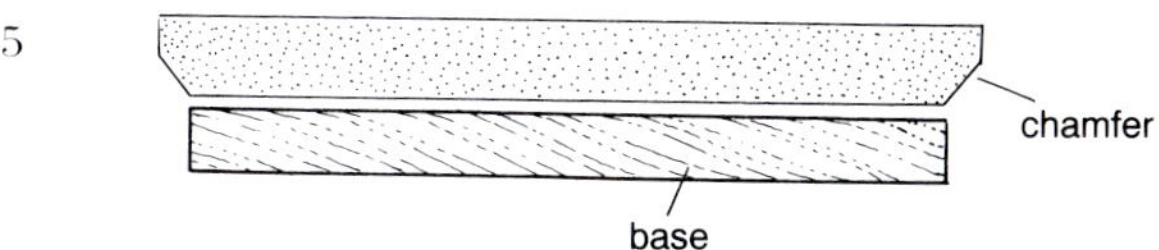

2 Mark the underside of the base into quarters. Place over the calico, having marked quarter positions, and line up with the base marks. Make sure that any protruding foam is pushed in so that the calico is flush against the edge of the base.

3 Staple the calico underneath the base, having pulled it over the foam to give a firm feel, but not so much that the foam is depressed: smoothing your hand over the calico should not produce any wrinkles. Staple the calico evenly at the quarter marks, then at approximately 1cm (⅜in) intervals in between (fig. 6). Trim the excess calico close to the staples.

6

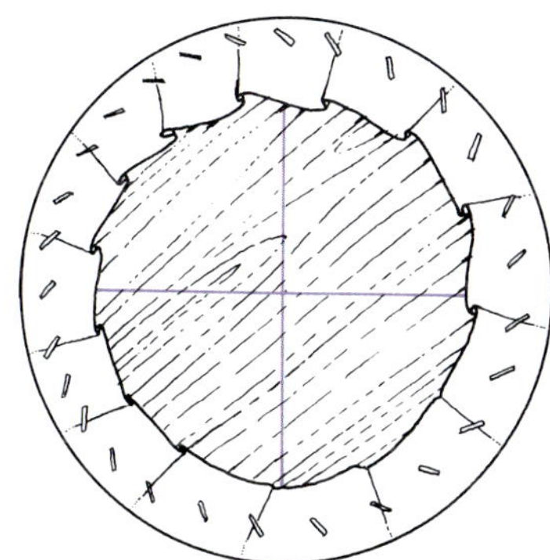

4 Place over the polyester wadding, then the needlepoint, having marked quarter positions. Attach again underneath and check that the tension is firm and that the gathers are evenly distributed around the edges without any pleats on the top side. You may find it helpful to insert a gathering thread of strong cotton about 2cm (¾in) from the stitched needlepoint before stapling. Trim excess canvas and place in the stool frame.

VARIATIONS

Most of the older footstools are not in this drop-in style, so that the needlepoint has to be attached to the main frame, either covering all edge wood and secured underneath (fig. 7), or tacked up to a show-wood band (fig. 8). For the former, a piece of bottoming is required to cover the raw edges of canvas and, for the latter, a trimming is necessary to hide the tacks or staples, and raw edges. Buy a commercial braid or, for a perfect colour match, use the needlepoint wools and make up the plaited braid described on page 23.

7

8

Musical Cherubs Piano Stool

Pin-cushion stool; traditional

As mentioned earlier, pin-cushion or pin-stuffed upholstery is thinly stuffed and padded to achieve a smooth, slimline effect. This type of upholstery was not only seen on chair back panels in Georgian times during the late 18th century, but also on the backs of sofas and couches in the Regency era of the early 19th century. However, it was not until the turn of the century that pin-cushion seats became abundant. Arts and Crafts designers, and later those of the Art Nouveau movement, delighted in simpler styles and lighter weight furniture, in which the shape, wood and finish of the chair frame took precedence over the upholstery.

Many chairs had both pin-cushion seats known as 'pad seats', as well as back panels, but were often so lightweight that they were only suitable for occasional use. At the same time, many reproductions of earlier styles were produced, including a good number to which pin-cushion upholstery could be applied. After this period, very little seating furniture was manufactured with pin-stuffed upholstery, probably because its fragilility is unsuitable for modern, everyday living.

To stitch the design

Finished size: 42 x 33.5cm (16½ x 13¼in)

MATERIALS

Materials are given for the size of chair above. To measure up for your own chair, see pages 98 and 109.

Canvas: 11hpi double, white, size 58 x 50cm (23 x 20in)

Thread: DMC tapestry wool in the following shades:

7175, 7472, 7503,	
7579, 7078, 7950,	
7144, 7452, 7453, 7141	*1 skein each*
7166, 7275	*2 skeins each*
7460	*3 skeins*
7520, écru	*4 skeins each*
7196	*5 skeins*
7147	*3½ hanks*

DMC light gold thread:

art 282	*1 reel*

Needle: tapestry size 18

Stitches: continental tent for the cherubs, music and border; basketweave for the background; using one strand of tapestry wool throughout except for cherubs' hair for which one strand of metallic thread is added to the wool

INSTRUCTIONS

Follow the chart on pages 56 and 57. Mark the centre of the canvas and stitch the four cherubs first. Where the metallic thread is indicated, cut only a short length and combine it with a similar length of wool. Stitch the music stave and notes, then the border pattern; complete by filling in the background with shade number 7147.

To adapt the design

A design with a musical theme, which has been reversed from the centre to make it multi-directional. Highlights in gold thread have been added to the cherubs' hair. The contrasting background is in dark red but could easily be changed to fit in with a different colour scheme.

1

2

- For a wider seat, stitch the border down both sides. For a larger seat, a double row of the border pattern can be used to increase the overall size by 5cm (2in) either at top and bottom (fig. 1) or on all sides. For a smaller-sized top, simply remove the border completely.

- For a double-size piano stool, repeat the middle cherub at both ends (fig. 2).

3

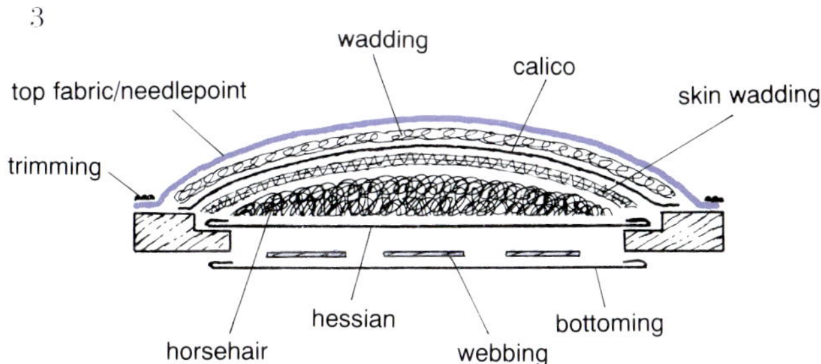

4

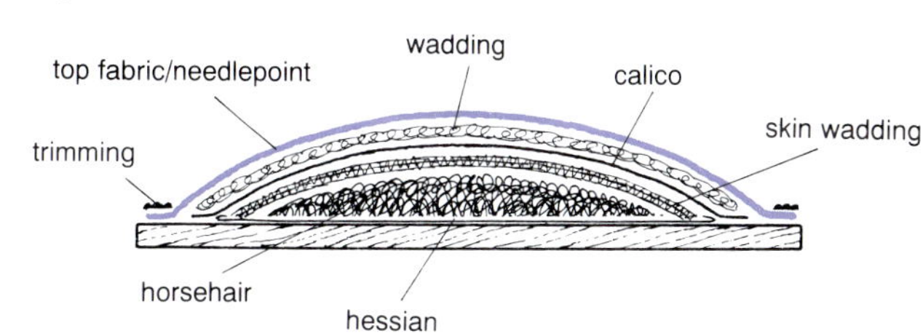

To upholster a pin-cushion seat using traditional methods and materials

Your pin-cushion stool should have a gently mounded shape, sloping down towards the wooden frame. The layers in the seat should be as shown in fig. 3.

This seat usually doubles up as a lid over a music storage area, and may well have a solid base. In this case, the layers would be as in fig. 4.

If the seat feels firm and is the right shape, it can have the needlepoint cover attached on top. If not, the chart on page 54 will help you to identify and deal with the problem.

Fault	*Remedy*
Broken webbing or sagging below the frame	Replace the webbing or tighten up (the upholstery will have to be removed to do this).
Holes or rips in the hessian	Strip down to the hessian and replace.
Hollow seat	If sagged webbing is the cause, you must remove all the upholstery; if not, then more stuffing is needed.
Lumpy seat	Replace stuffing or, if old horsehair, re-tease and add some more.
Wrong size/shape	Adjust the amount of stuffing.
The entire upholstery has come away from the frame	There will be insufficient tacking space, so repair the wooden frame with wood glue mixed with fine saw-dust. Re-upholster using the additional tips opposite or, alternatively, re-upholster using foam and staples (see page 22) as this will place less strain on the frame.

MATERIALS (for complete re-upholstering)

Black and white webbing: 1.5m (5ft); omit if the lid has a solid base
12oz hessian: 44 x 35cm (17 x 14in)
Mattress twine: 2m (6ft)
Horsehair stuffing: 0.25-0.5kg (½-¾lb)
Skin wadding: 41 x 33cm (16 x 13in)
Calico: 45 x 37cm (18 x 14¼in)
Polyester wadding: 41 x 33cm (16 x 13in)
Fine tacks: 13mm (½in) and 10mm (⅜in)
Trimming: 1.4m (4ft 9in) gimp or braid
Glue: clear fabric adhesive
Matching gimp pins

METHOD

1 Web and tack hessian on the top of the frame using 13mm (½in) fine tacks.

2 Make bridle loops flat on the hessian. Place the stuffing under the loops, with slightly more in the centre and letting the depth gradually fall away so that it forms a rounded shape.

3 Lie the skin wadding over the stuffing and attach the calico with 10mm (⅜in) fine tacks. Try to graduate the position of each layer on the tacking rail.

4 Stretch the needlepoint over a layer of polyester wadding, folding under the excess canvas before tacking down. Pleats should not be necessary at the corners, as the needlepoint should smooth away gradually. Attach the gimp or braid.

ADDITIONAL TIPS FOR PIN-CUSHION SEATS

1 A cabriole headed hammer, which has a small head and is lighter in weight, will help to avoid damaging the show-wood on the lid.

2 Dab a small amount of glue under the webbing ends and folded hessian edges for extra security.

3 Ensure that the stuffing or wadding does not extend beyond the tacking line, as this will cause unsightly bumps.

4 Gimp pins, with their small heads and slim shanks, can be used instead of the 10mm (⅜in) fine tacks to attach the needlepoint and even the calico, if there is little space for tacking.

5 Horsehair stuffing, rather than fibre, is better here because it is finer and more likely to give a smoother shape and feel to the seat.

London

Victorian Prie-Dieu Chair

Needlepoint panels; traditional

Also known as vesper or devotional chairs, this style was first seen in the 1820s but, by the 1850s, began to go out of fashion. It was intended for kneeling on, not sitting, with the upholstered platform at the top of the back providing a resting area for arms and hands while praying or for a prayer book. These chairs provided an ideal opportunity for the 'ladies of the house' to stitch and display their Berlin woolwork, both as an all-over covering or as a bordered panel, as in this project. Designs were mostly floral, although many also had a more religious nature. It is interesting to note how the background colours changed through the decades: from soft pastels in the early 1820s to dark green, blue and black in the1850s, finishing with sludgy brown and dull burgundy.

The stitched needlepoint panel is a traditional design for this chair, both in colours and content. Lilies, along with fuchsias and amaryllis, were the new conservatory or 'hot house' flowers grown in the mid-19th century, and soon found their way into needlepoint patterns. The dark green background firmly dates the design to the 1850s.

To stitch the design

Finished size: back panel, 84 x 19cm (33 x 7½in)
seat panel, 59 x 19cm (23¼ x 7½in)

MATERIALS

Materials are given for the size of panels above. To measure for your own chair, make the panel between a third and a half the overall width of the chair.

Canvas: 11hpi double white, 2 pieces in sizes 100 x 35cm (39⅜ x 13¾in) and 75 x 35cm (29½ x 13¾in)

Thread: DMC tapestry wool in the following shades:

7579, 7422	*2 skeins each*
7115	*3 skeins*
7193, 7196	*4 skeins each*
7951, 7351, 7200	*5 skeins each*
7179, 7364, 7583	*6 skeins each*
7758	*7 skeins*
7194	*8 skeins*
écru	*2 hanks*
7398	*6 hanks*

Needle: tapestry size 18

Stitches: continental tent for the lilies, stalks and leaves; basketweave for the background; using one strand of wool throughout

repeat
repeat
7951
7179
7196
7579
ecru
7200
7194
7758
7351
7583
7364
7115
7422
7193
7398

INSTRUCTIONS

Follow the chart on page 60. The back requires about three and a half of the pattern repeats. These have been positioned so that a full repeat starts underneath the top of the back, two full pattern repeats are then placed centrally down the front (fig. 1). Start stitching at the top of the canvas, stamens first, petals second, followed by the leaves and stalks, and finishing with the background worked in shade number 7398. Depending on the size of the frame, complete as large a section as possible before starting the next.

The lily repeats on the seat are positioned to match up with the back panel and produce a continuous pattern. This placing has also given a full repeat approximately in the centre of the seat. Start stitching 14cm (5½in) above the beginning of the repeat (marked on the chart) and continue through one whole pattern and 22cm (8⅝in) into the next (see fig. 2). Stitch in the same order as for the back panel. Remove from the frame and block back to shape if necessary.

To attach a needlepoint panel

1 Attach flies or extensions to the top and bottom edges of both needlepoint panels: these are pieces of fabric sewn to the edges to economise on covering fabric. This was often practised in Victorian times, when the cost of fabric far exceeded the cost of labour. They are used in this project to provide a strong fabric for pulling and tacking, in place of the canvas already weakened by blocking and stretching. Use a strong fabric - for example, heavyweight calico - and add pieces about 5cm (2in) long at the top of the back and front of the seat, and 10cm (4in) long at the bottom of the back and back of the seat. The extra length on the last two edges will then be sufficient to reach the back tacking rail (fig. 3).

2 Measure and cut out the plain fabric for either side of both panels, adding on an appropriate amount for seam allowances (fig. 4). Note that the back pieces need only go round onto the sides of the chair, not the back, as a separate side panel is to be attached.

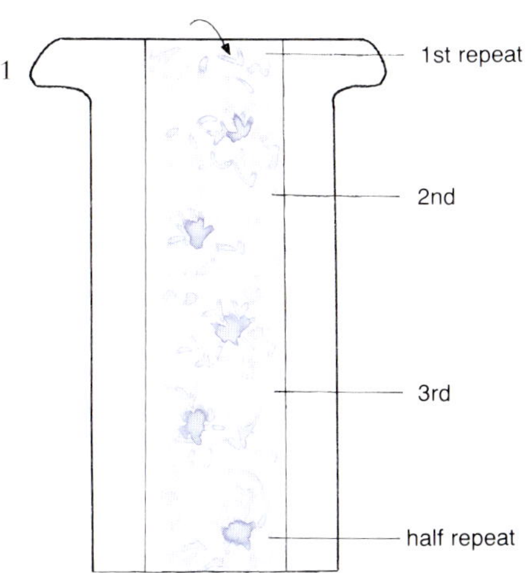

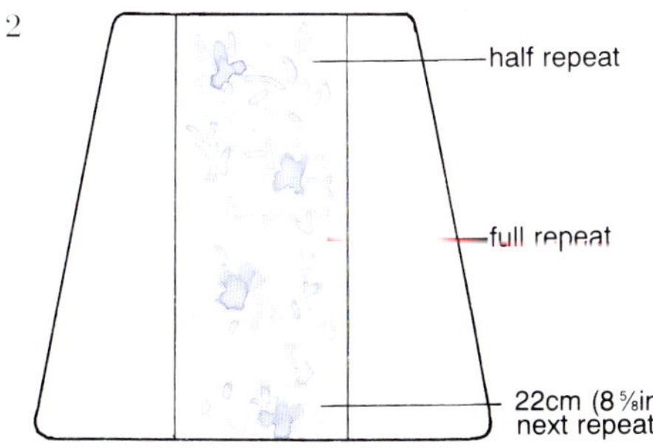

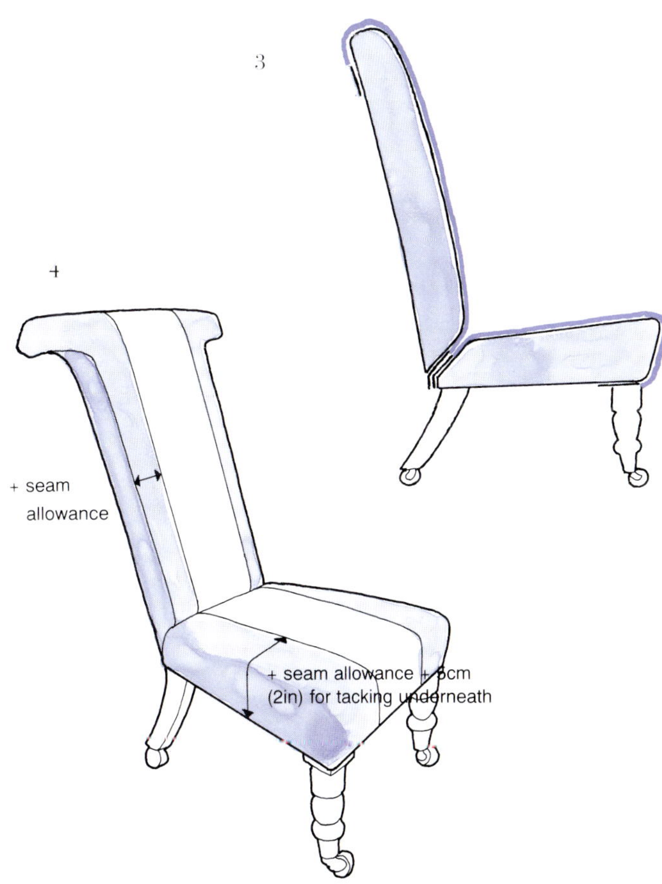

3 The join between the needlepoint panels and the border fabric is usually enhanced with a decorative cord or piping. Cords can be flanged - that is, with a tape attached to the cord which acts in the same way as piping - or you can use a single cord. If using a flanged cord or piping, it must be sewn onto the needlepoint panel before attaching to the border fabric. A piping foot is recommended as this will eliminate any slipping of the layers while sewing. Pin and tack the layers first, so that all the unstitched canvas is covered. Machine stitch the fabric borders to the needlepoint as close as possible to the cord or piping. Press the seam allowances towards the border fabric; if using velvet, press very lightly so that the pile is not damaged.

4 The made-up back and seat pieces can now be attached to the chair. Start with the seat, tacking to achieve a firm tension, before folding tight pleats at the corners.

5 Attach the back panel along the top tacking rail and down through to the back of the seat, positioning the needlepoint panel centrally. Skewer the fabric to the sides of the front, adjusting their positions until the tension is tight. Cut into the inside corners of the platform so that the fabric can stretch around the corner edges (fig. 5). Take care not to over-cut as this will be visible from the front. Stitch with a blind stitch underneath the roll edge using a small curved needle and a fine linen or button thread (fig. 6).

6 Position the border fabric with skewers turning in the seam allowances. Tack to the back of the frame and ladder stitch to the fabric, including the two joins where the top and side borders meet.

7 Attach the outside back panel by back tacking the top edge with back tacking strip (fig. 7). Cover over the back space with calico or hessian for reinforcement, before pulling down the fabric and tacking under the seat. Fold in the seam allowance on the sides, pin in position and ladder stitch. Tidy up the underneath of the seat by attaching a piece of bottoming.

UPHOLSTERY INSTRUCTIONS

The upholstery of this chair repeats methods and materials used in other projects: the back requires the same method as for a top-stuffed seat on page 33 and the seat that of the sprung stool on page 41, but with only five springs. Work the back first.

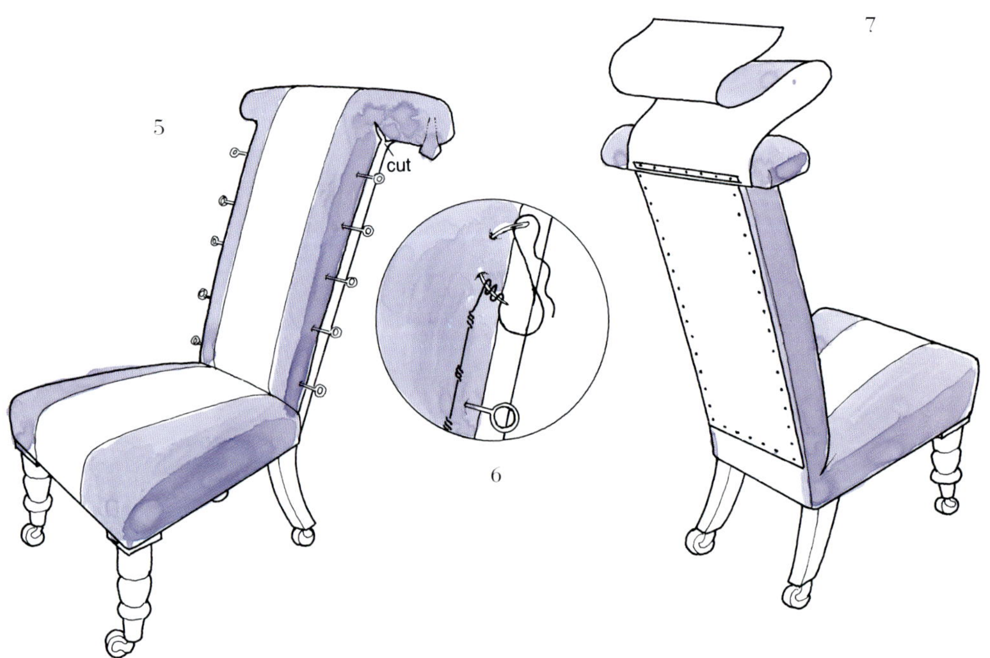

To adapt the design

• A shorter or longer length of needlepoint can easily be achieved by altering the overall number of repeat patterns. However, the starting point for the stitching may need to be changed in order that a full pattern repeat remains centralised on the seat or back area.

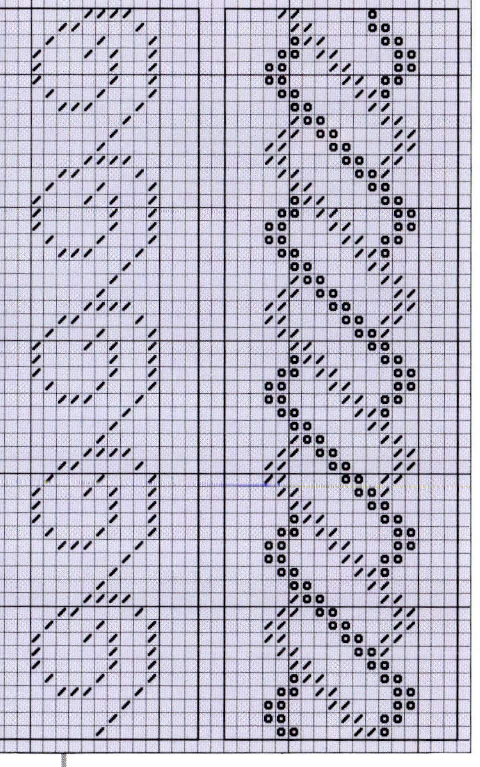

8

• The width of the lily panel is 19cm (7½in), but could be increased with the addition of a border each side, if the size of the chair warrants it. Suggestions for suitable borders are shown in the photograph in a variety of possible colourways.

• This design could become an all-over pattern if preferred, by repeating the panel of lilies. Place one panel in the centre, then one on both sides, positioning them as half-drops (fig. 8). Additional panels can be added on until an entire surface is fully covered.

Peony and Lotus Flower Box

Padded box; modern

Box ottomans or padded boxes have been used both for occasional seating and for providing storage since the 18th century. The word 'ottoman' originated in Turkey, the definition being 'a low wide upholstered bench without a back'. In the early 19th century, during the Regency period, these boxes were upholstered in the simple, classical style of the day: that is, in plain and striped silks, with hair-filled mattress cushions. In the mid-late 19th century, however, the Victorians used elaborate upholstery with curvaceous padding, deep buttoning, tufting, needlepoint, beadwork and highly decorative trimmings.

The 20th century saw a new version of the ottoman: the Lloyd Loom boxes, with padded lids only. Today, padded boxes are as popular as ever.

In this project a padded border for the lid is made to frame a needlepoint panel.

The tab for opening the lid is made from a buckram base, covered with needlepoint. Perlé cotton has been chosen for the canvas-work because of its lovely lustre and sheen, and it is worked on a fine 15 gauge canvas to achieve the desired detail in the design.

To stitch the design

Finished needlepoint size: 33 x 23cm (13 x 9in)
Box size: 46 x 35.5 x 35.5 (height) cm (18 x 14 x 14in)

MATERIALS

Canvas: 15 hpi, double thread, white, two pieces: 41 x 31cm (16 x12 in) and 16 x 11cm (7 x 5in)
Thread: DMC perlé cotton, thickness 5 in the following shades:

351, 352, 353, 356, 502, 504, 518, 597, 598, 676, 746, 758, 932, 945, 948, 955	*1 skein each*
931	*2 skeins*
écru	*4 skeins*

Needle: tapestry size 20
Stitches: half cross stitch throughout; using one strand of perlé cotton

INSTRUCTIONS

This is the only project where durability has not been an essential requirement. An alternative to wool has been selected, as has a different type of stitch. Half cross stitch is finer and less bulky than the usual needlepoint stitches; desirable qualities in keeping with the silk covering. Follow the chart on pages 68 and 69. Mark the centre of the canvas, then count the threads and mark the inside border line. Start stitching the gold coloured outlines of the central peony first, filling these in before moving on to complete all the flowers and leaves. The border pattern can be worked next, and finally the two background areas worked in écru. Stitch the tab in the same way, following the chart on page 72.

To adapt the design

The needlepoint panel displays traditional, stylised flowers and leaves, which are still much used in China, particularly on textiles and costumes. The peony symbolises 'wealth and honour' and the lotus flower 'purity in a sinful world'.
As boxes can vary so much in size and shape, this design - with its randomly patterned border - can be easily adapted.

• For a much smaller box, just a portion of the main design could be stitched, the central peony, for example (fig. 1) or, for an even smaller box, the lotus flower (fig. 2).

• Numerous patterns can be made up by repeating and reversing parts of the design, achieving a variety of overall shapes (fig. 3 and fig. 4). Use tracing paper over the outline of the motif on the chart and experiment until you are satisfied with the result. However, only turn the design outlines through 90, 180, or 270 degrees, so that the existing chart can be worked from.

2

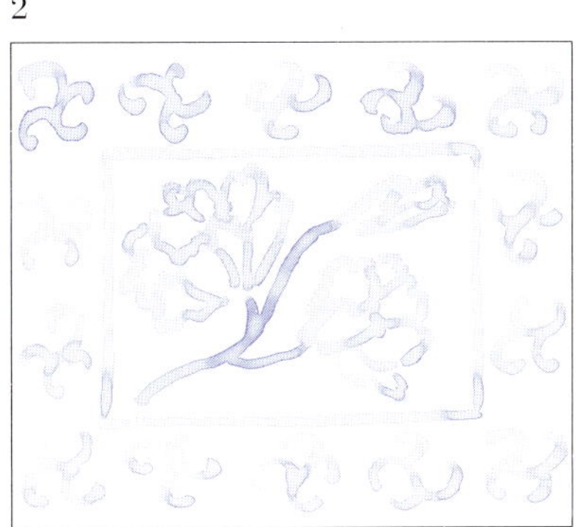

4

1

3

To upholster a padded box using modern methods and materials

The materials used for your box will depend not only on its age and style, but also on how expensive it was when produced. Fillings may vary from horsehair to straw. As styles of boxes varied, so too did the upholstery techniques used; for faults and remedies refer to the appropriate chapter for your type, e.g. refer to page 41 for a sprung lid box.

A problem peculiar to padded boxes is the slipping of the padding on the sides, so that the top part feels empty and the lower half lumpy and uneven. If this does not need replacing and is a sheet material, such as skin wadding, place very small dabs of glue onto the sides and pull up the wadding. If the padding is loose, for example, horsehair, it has probably slipped through the bridle loops. Remove, making sure the loops lie vertically not horizontally, then re-stuff. If the padding is to be replaced, several sheets of skin wadding are ideal, or use the more modern polyester wadding.

MATERIALS (for complete re-upholstering)

Chalk pencil or light sensitive fabric marker pencil
2.5cm (1in) combustion modified, medium grade foam: 2 pieces, 48 x 37.5cm (19 x 14¾ in) and 33 x 22.5cm (13 x 9in)
Top covering fabric*: 1.4m (4ft 6in)
4oz polyester wadding: 1.5m (5ft)
Muslin/lining fabric for quilting: 46cm (18in), 122cm (48in) wide
Matching sewing thread
Medium piping cord: 1m (3ft 3in)
Calico: two strips 18cm (7in) wide x 55cm (21¾in); two strips 18 x 45 cm (7 x 17¾in); one piece 38 x 28cm (15 x 19in)
Back tacking strip: 2m (6ft 6in)
Staples: 10 or 13mm (⅜ or ½in) for all stapling and 6mm (¼in) for the lid panel only
Glue: rubber-based plus contact adhesive
2oz polyester wadding: 3m (9¾ft)
Small curved needle
Inside lining fabric*: 1.5m (5ft), 122cm (48in) wide
Bottoming (black): 38 x 48cm (15 x 19in)
Two pieces of thin cardboard: 45 x 35.5cm (17¾ x 14in) and 42 x 32.5cm (16½ x 12¾in)
6mm plywood: 31 x 20.5cm (12¼ x 8in)
Buckram: 12 x 7cm (5 x 3in)

Materials are given for the size of box on page 64. For your own box, measure the front and side panels together, with a separate back panel for the top fabric. For the inside lining, measure each side separately. Add 5cm (2in) on all sides of each piece.

METHOD

Covering fabric layout (fig. 5) and lining fabric layout (fig. 6).

5

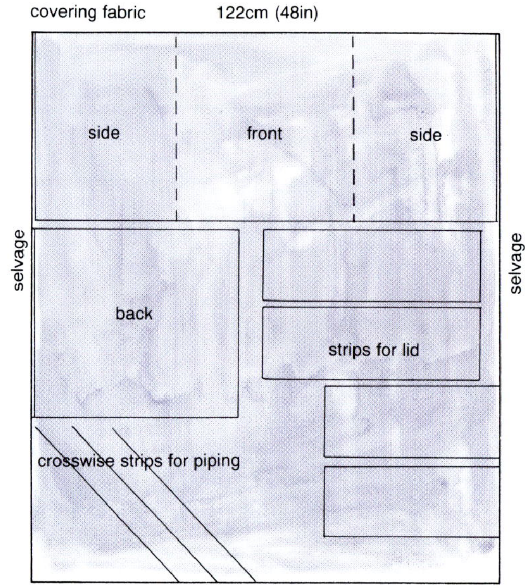

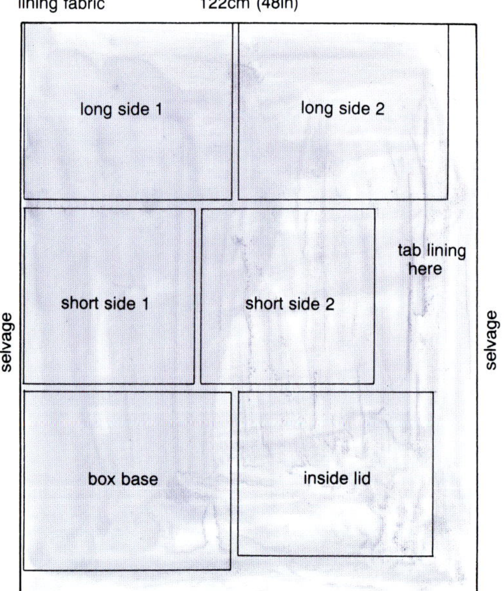

6

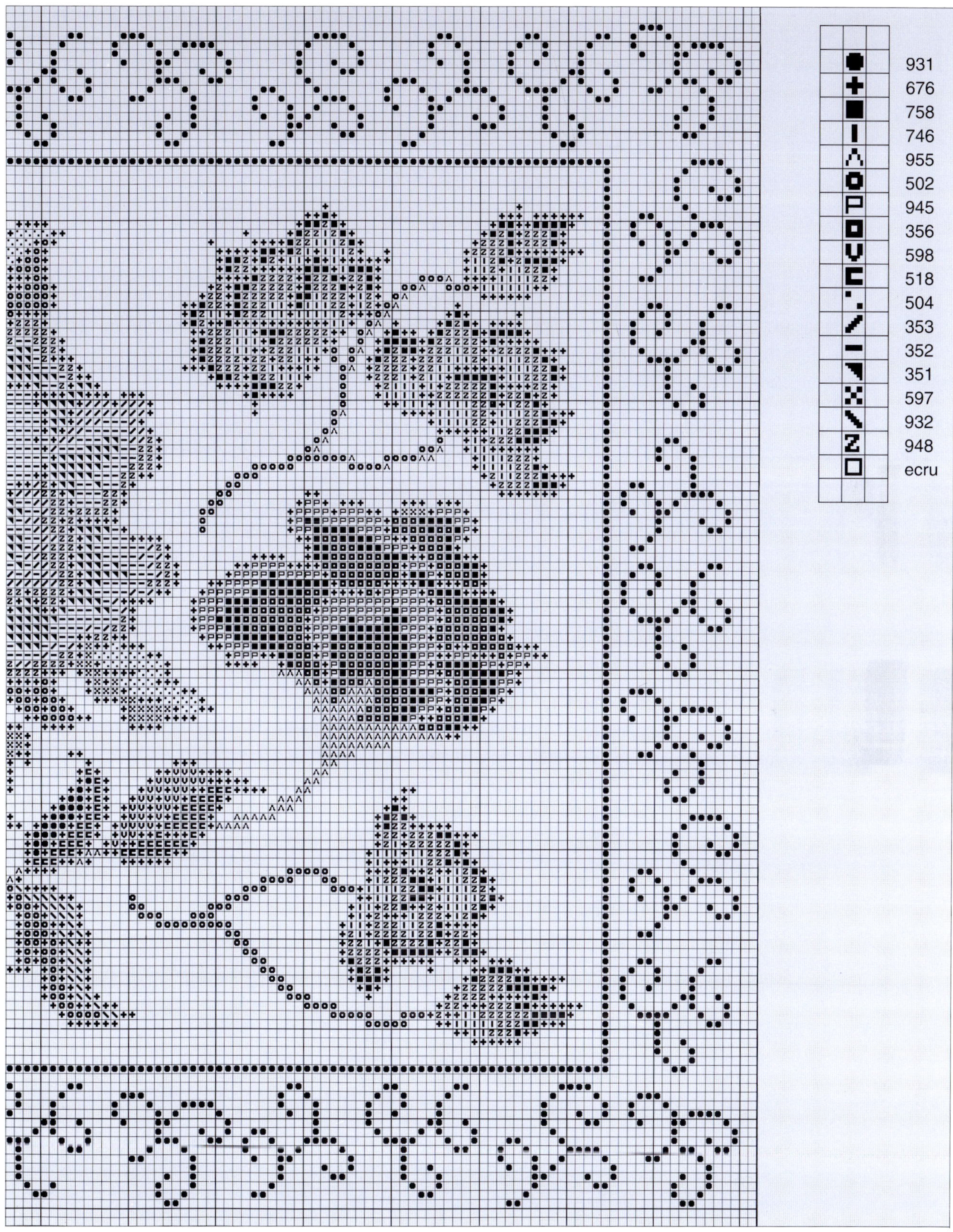
931
676
758
746
955
502
945
356
598
518
504
353
352
351
597
932
948
ecru

Sides of the Box

1 First remove the hinges. Draw the quilting outline onto the covering fabric for the front and sides using the template (fig. 7, page 72) and a chalk pencil or light sensitive fabric marker pencil. Randomly position these all over the front, gradually fading away around the sides.

2 Layer this fabric on top of the 4oz polyester wadding with the lining/muslin underneath. Tack to hold together (fig. 8).

3 Machine-quilt with the matching sewing thread, remove the tacking and tidy the loose ends, then place on the box. Staple in position at the top and bottom first, then bring the seam allowance onto the back and staple. Pleat the fabric over the top of the corners (fig. 9).

4 Attach the two lengths of covered piping by stapling along the back panel edges, so that they protrude slightly (fig. 10).

5 Dab a small amount of glue onto the back of the box and place a piece of 4oz polyester wadding cut to the same width as the back panel plus 1cm (½in) extra, top and bottom. Place over the top fabric and staple at top and bottom, as for the front panel. Fold in the side edges and pin, then ladder stitch with a small curved needle, close up to the piping (fig. 11).

6 Back tack the inside lining along the upper edge of each long side (fig. 12). Attach the 2oz wadding to these sides with a small amount of glue, then fold over the fabric and staple to the inside box base.

7 Repeat for the short sides, folding in the extra fabric (fig. 13).

8 Cover the large piece of cardboard with the layer of 2oz wadding, then the lining fabric, gluing this to the underside of the card. Place in the bottom of the box. Attach bottoming to complete.

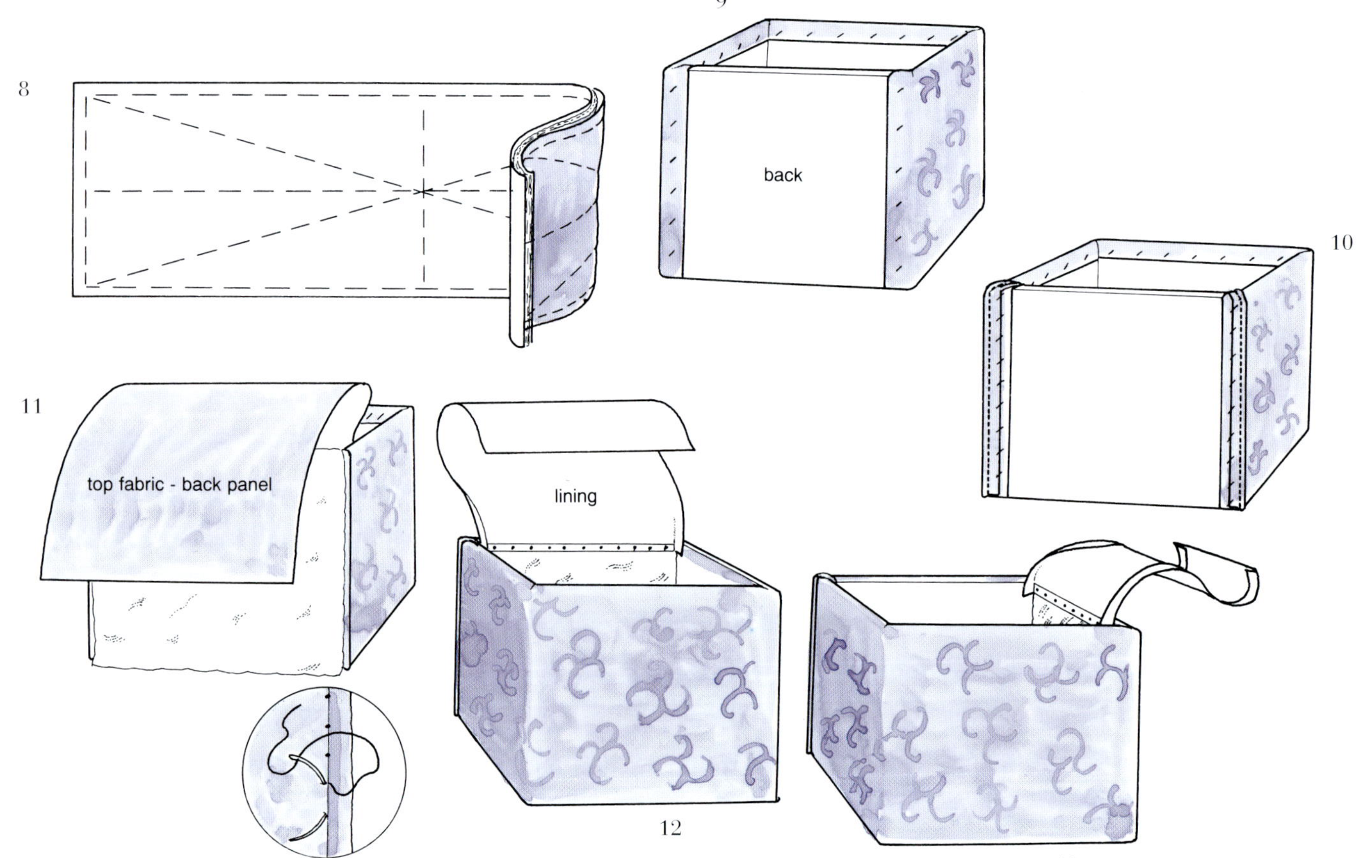

A close-up detail of the peony and lotus design worked in cotton perlé

Windsor-Style Rocking Chair

Mattress cushion; traditional

This type of cushion provides a substantial seat pad for a lovely rocking chair and should retain its shape for many years. The cover is bordered and piped, while the inner ticking case is filled with horsehair and stitched to hold it in place. These mattress cushions have been made and used for centuries, long before any foam or springs were developed. As early as medieval times, they provided comfort on hard wooden seats and towards the end of the 17th century were seen over the caned bases of many William & Mary chairs.

As fixed upholstery became more commonplace, these cushions were used on many Chippendale and Hepplewhite sofas. During the early 19th century, they were particularly suitable for the late Regency day beds, settees, and ottomans, when squareness and angularity were the vogue.

The needlepoint design of ripe pears against a bright tartan background is especially suitable for this country-style chair. It is stitched on a large gauge canvas of 8hpi with double tapestry wool, making it a very quick and simple project.

To stitch the design

Finished size: depth, 44cm (17¼in)
back width, 34cm (13⅜in)
front width, 42cm (16½in)

MATERIALS

Materials are given for the size of cushion above. To measure the canvas for a different size, make a template as described on page 77 (step 1) and add an extra 5cm (2in) of unstitched canvas on all sides.

Canvas: 8hpi, double thread, white; 54 x 52cm (21¼ x 20½in)

Thread: Appletons tapestry wools in the following shades:

477, 866, 992, 472, 766, 904	*1 skein each*
252, 996, 864, 254, 255, 253	*2 skeins each*
474, 843, 855	*3 skeins each*
872, 472, 251A	*1 hank each*
322	*4 hanks*

Needle: tapestry size 16

Stitches: continental tent for pears, leaves, checks; basketweave for checked background; using double tapestry wool throughout.

INSTRUCTIONS

Follow the chart on page 78. Mark the centre of the canvas and work the leaves first, then the pears, using the centre mark on the chart to help with positioning. For the background, stitch the lines first to the required width and depth, taking care to work the correct 'under and over' positions. Finally, fill in between the lines with shade number 322, starting at the top and working downwards.

To adapt the design

• Different sizes of chair seat are not a problem with this design, as the amount of tartan background can be easily increased or reduced. It is likely, however, that a small version will be required, perhaps for an average-sized kitchen chair. A preferable alternative to reducing the background to almost nothing is to stitch the complete project on a smaller gauge canvas, with single tapestry wool. An 11 gauge, when stitched, would have an approximate finished size of 33 x 31cm (13 x 12¼in).

• Other likely uses for this cushion are for a window seat, settle or pew. For these, the fruit motif can be repeated as many times as necessary. Make a template of the required cushion size, then cut out and place several circles of about 23cm (9in) on the template to represent the fruit, and decide on the exact positions and number of repeats. Remember that the fruit can only be placed at 90, 180, or 270 degree angles, because of the canvas grid. It is advisable to draw one vertical and one horizontal line through the cut out circles, and match these to the canvas grid lines, whatever direction the pears may be lying in (fig. 1).

1

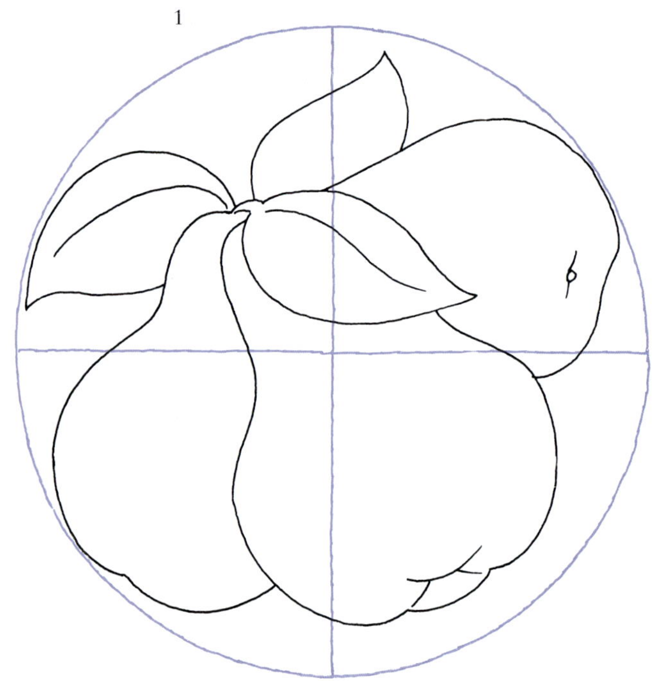

To make the mattress cushion

Finished size: same as the needlepoint panel, with a raised border of 2.5cm (1in). Any existing cushion should feel firm and have a level surface, with upright walls or borders. Possible problems are shown on the next page.

MATERIALS (for a new cushion)

Black and white ticking: 0.6m (23⅝in), 137cm (54in) wide
Matching sewing thread for ticking and outer fabric
Horsehair: 0.75kg (1½lb)
Mattress needle: fine 15cm (6in)
Strong linen thread
2.5cm (1in) diameter circles of soft leather/suede: 15
Strong cotton fabric in a co-ordinating colour: 0.5m (20in)
Piping cord: medium thickness, 2m (6½ft)

Fault	*Remedy*
Mis-shapen with a sunken middle seat section	The stuffing has compressed over the years and must be removed and discarded, unless horsehair. This can be washed, dried, and re-teased, with a little extra added to compensate for any that has broken up .
Ticking cover in poor repair: e.g. worn holes or rips, disintegrating, and very stained	A new cover is needed, as the ticking has simply worn out with age and use. It is also likely that the stuffing will need replacing or cleaning.

METHOD

Inner Case and Pad

1 Cut a paper template to the exact shape required for the finished cushion. Measure round the template for the border, which here is 2.5cm (1in); but can be made larger if preferred.

2 Cut two pieces of ticking for the top and bottom panels 2cm (¾in) larger than the template on all sides. This 2cm (¾in) allows a 1.5cm (⅝in) seam allowance and 0.5cm (¼in) for the 'take-up' required by the tufting ties (fig. 2).

3 Cut the border in one piece if possible, adding 1.5cm (⅝in) seam allowance to sides and ends (fig. 2). Stitch short ends together.

4 Machine stitch border to bottom panel, right sides facing, leaving a hand-size opening in one of the back seams. When attaching the border, notch the corners on the top and bottom edges - they can then be placed in the same position on both panels (fig. 3). This ensures that the border is attached squarely. Next stitch border to top panel, right sides together. Turn right side out.

5 Stuff the cushion firmly, ensuring that there is an adequate amount around the edges and in

2

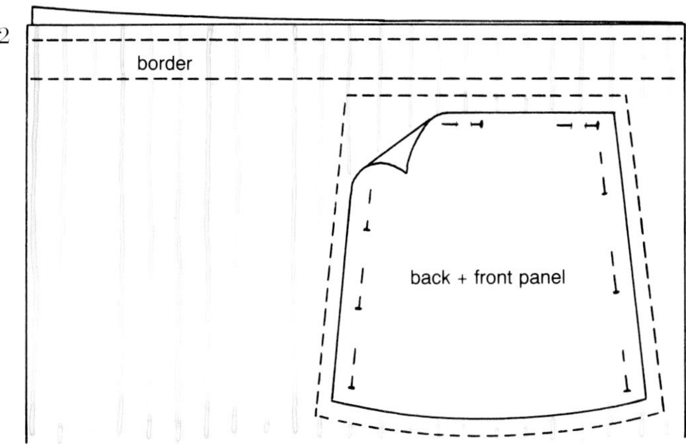

3

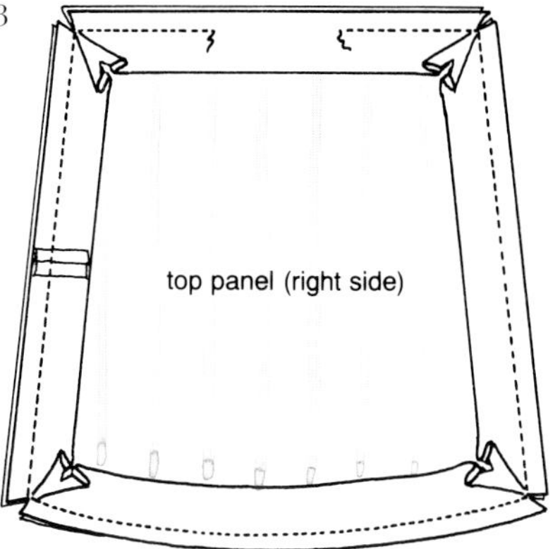

4

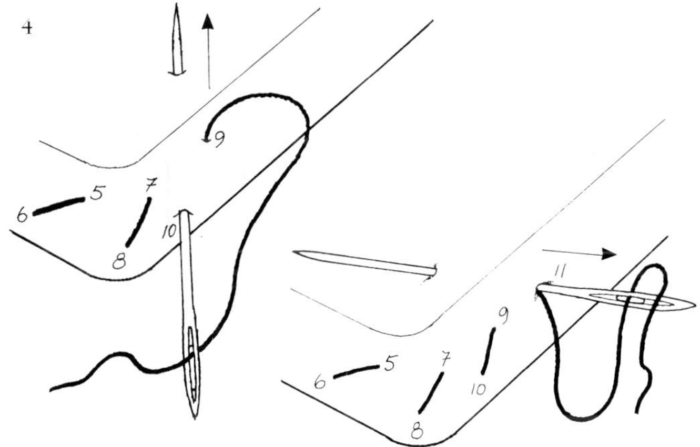

the corners. Keep the overall shape flat and not mounded in the centre. Close the opening with slip stitching.

6 Using the mattress needle and linen thread, stitch two rows of 'box stitch' around the borders (fig. 4). If the band is narrow, that is,

Symbol	Colour	Symbol	Colour
◢	766	O	477
N	251A	⊠	864
=	472	\	474
I	872	C	843
•	996	U	252
∧	253	T	992
+	254	/	855
⋱	255	●	866
■	904	□	322

A close-up detail of the needlepoint for the mattress cushion

2.5cm (1in) or less, one row of stitching will be sufficient. The box stitch strengthens the edges by holding the stuffing in place, so that the cushion retains its shape.

7 Finish by inserting ties through the stuffing from top to bottom and attaching the leather circles (fig. 5) using the mattress needle and linen thread. Place about 12cm (4¾in) apart in squares and tightened up with an upholsterer's knot (fig. 6).

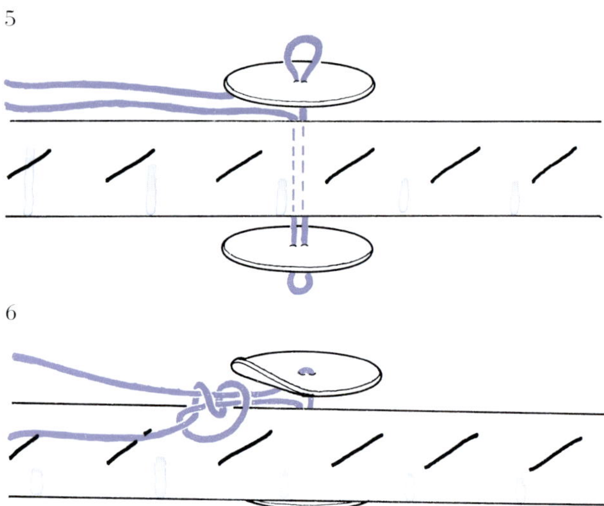

Outer Case

1 Cut out the bottom panel from the cotton fabric using the template and adding 1.5cm (⅝in) seam allowance. Cut the border to the same size as the ticking.

2 Check that the needlepoint is square and not distorted; if necessary, block back to shape, then trim the unstitched canvas to 1.5cm (⅝in).

3 Make up the required length of piping and attach to the right side of the needlepoint. Tack first, then machine stitch, taking care that all unstitched canvas is covered and that the stitching does not encroach on the needlepoint. Join up the piping ends neatly.

4 Attach the border to the needlepoint, with right sides together, but stop machining about 5cm (2in) away from the ends (fig. 7). Seam the border together, then sew the remaining part to the needlepoint. This ensures that the border fits perfectly.

5 Notch the four corners of the border as for the ticking (step 4 of the inner case instructions).

6 Attach the bottom panel, leaving a substantial opening along the entire back edge and around the corners (fig. 8). This size of opening is necessary

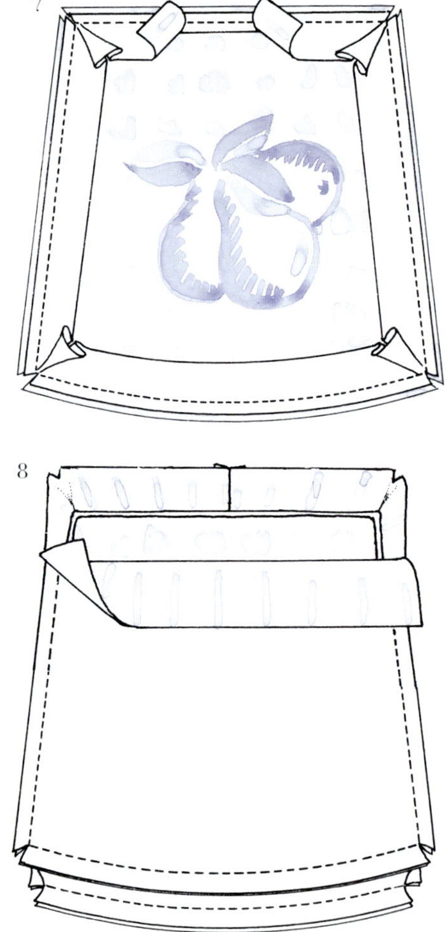

as the mattress cushion pad will not bend to be inserted. Finish by slip stitching the opening.

Child's Wicker Chair Cushion

Squab cushion; modern

To stitch the design

Finished size: depth, 32cm (12⅝in)
width, 30.5cm (12in)

MATERIALS

Materials are given for the size of cushion above. To measure the canvas for a different size, make a paper template of the required shape, then add 5cm (2in) on all sides for the border of unstitched canvas. Alternatively, measure the existing cushion and add the extra border as above.

Canvas: 10hpi double thread, white, size 42 x 41cm (16½ x 16⅛in)

Thread: DMC Broder Médicis crewel wool in the following shades:

8896, navy	*3 skeins each*
8567, 8904, 8995, 8997	*9 skeins each*

Needle: tapestry size 18

Stitches: cross stitch throughout; using three strands of crewel wool

This cushion is reasonably flat as it consists of two pieces of fabric joined together with piping, omitting the boxed edge. It is also softer than the mattress cushion (page 75) as its pad is made from modern polyester foam.

The development of plastic polyester foam in the 1950s, as well as new forms of springing, soon led to the widespread manufacture of foam seating cushions. The obvious advantages are its flexibility, that it is clean and easy to use, its speed in assembly and its lower cost compared to latex foam. The foam in this cushion was first wrapped with polyester wadding to soften the edges, then encased in stockinette, before being placed into the needlepoint cover.

The design of the needlepoint features our much loved feline friend, while the background is made up of simple checks, randomly decorated with stripes and swirls. Cross stitch is used, rather than tent or basketweave stitch, in order to give continuous outlines for the cats. Distortion of the canvas is also kept to a minimum with cross stitch, which is important when a piece of needlepoint is not secured permanently to a frame or base.

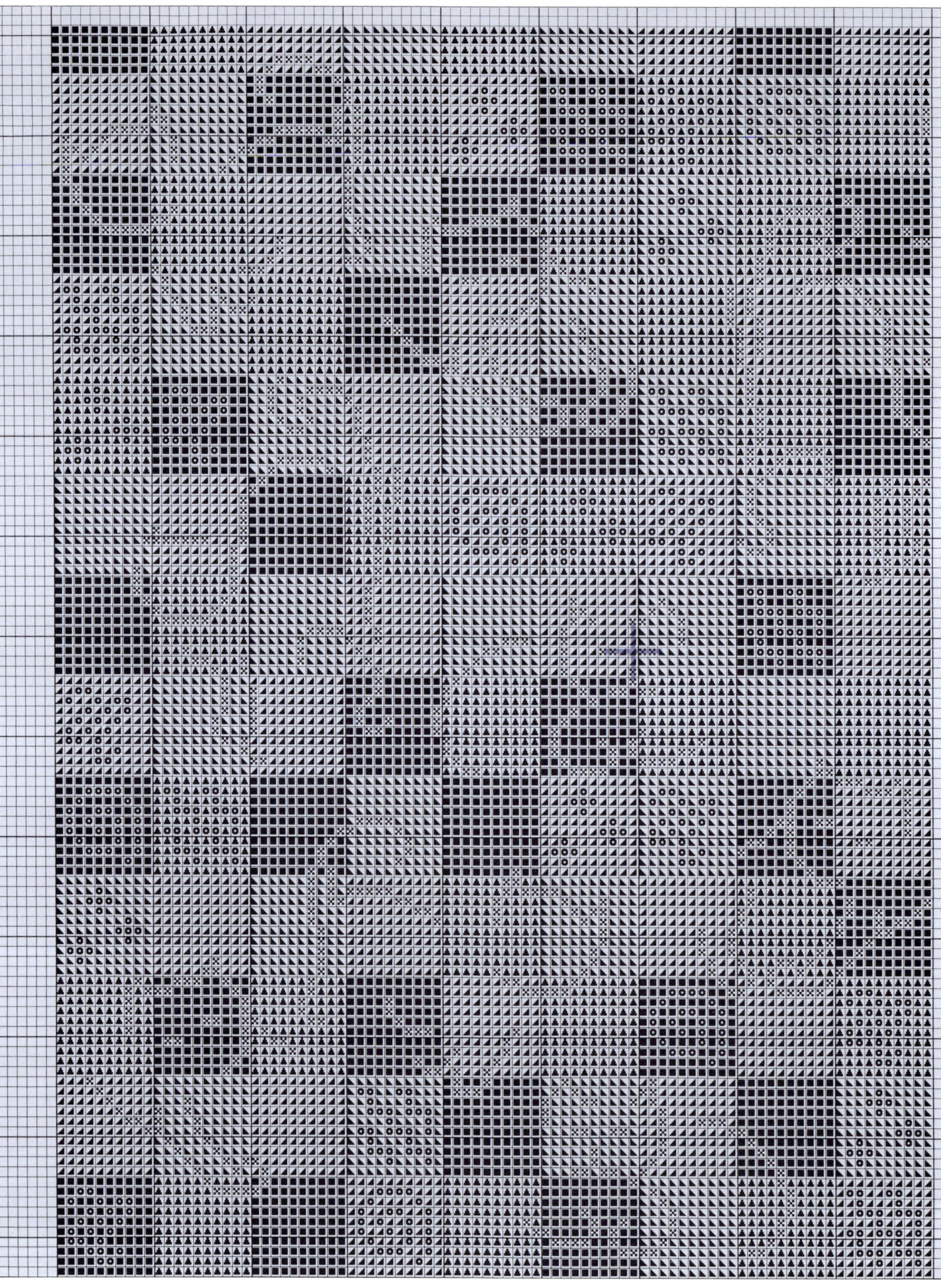

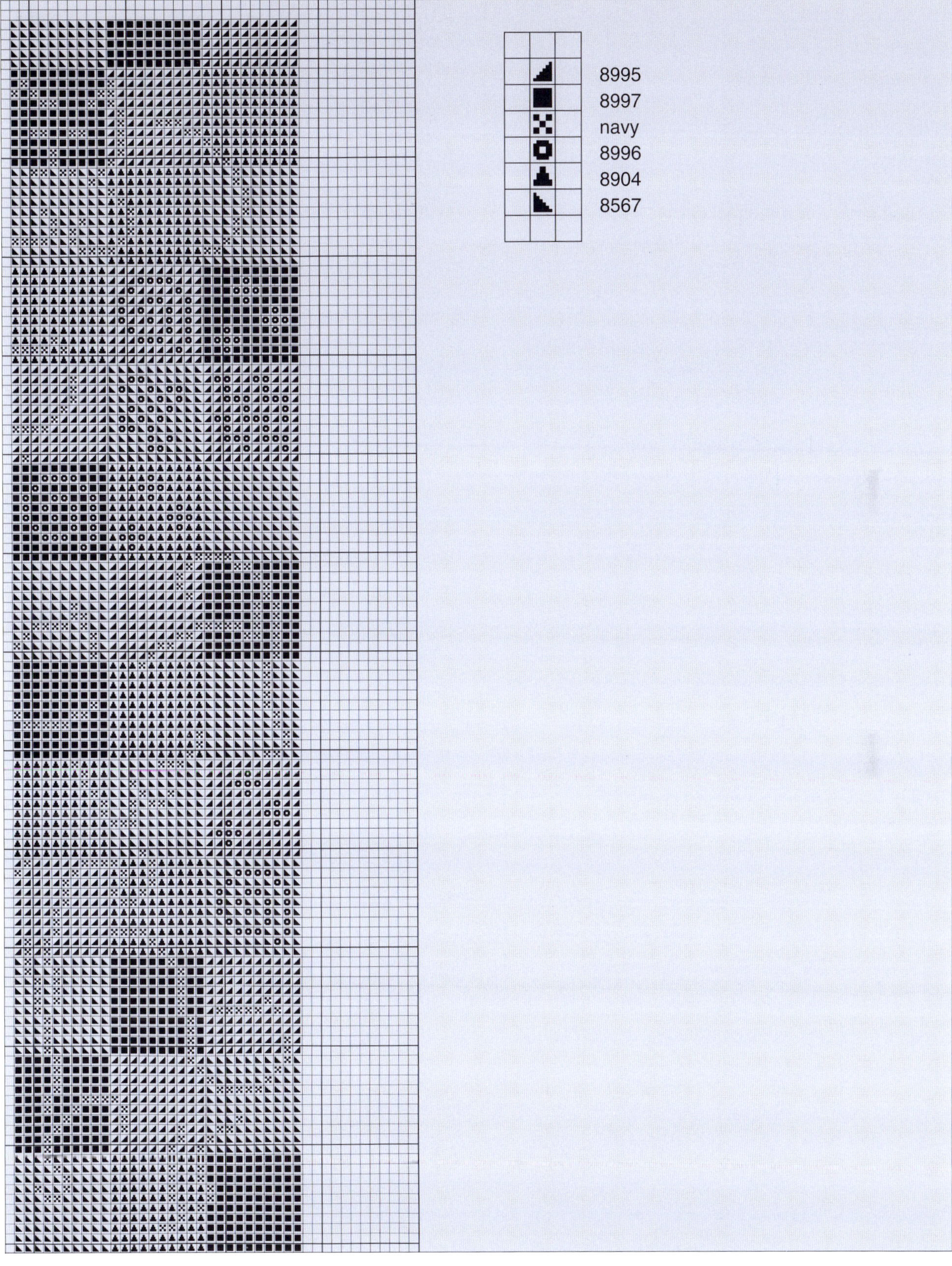
8995
8997
navy
8996
8904
8567

INSTRUCTIONS

Follow the chart on pages 84 and 85. Draw a ten thread grid onto the canvas; these lines should lie between two canvas threads and will make the positioning of the cats and blocks much easier. First stitch the cats in the navy wool, then the patterns on the blocks and finally the background, starting at the top and working downwards. As cross stitch does not distort the canvas, a frame is not essential; this means that the stitching can be speeded up by inserting the needle in two holes of the canvas at a time (fig 4, page 92). Try out both this method and the usual one with a frame, and select the one you prefer.

To make the squab cushion

Finished size is the same as for the needlepoint panel.

Any existing cushion on the chair should be the correct size and shape with a certain degree of resilience. Different problems may exist due to the fillings used:

Fault	*Remedy*
Completely flat without any springiness	Polyurethane foam compresses with use, so you need to replace it.
Lumpy and uneven	Latex foam disintegrates with exposure to light. Replace with polyurethane foam.
Mis-shapen	Hair or fibre will flatten and become distorted with constant use. Either replace or clean and re-tease old stuffing before re-using.

MATERIALS (for a new cushion)

2.5cm (1in) flame retardant foam: seating density, size 33 x 31.5 cm (13 x 12⅜in)
2oz polyester wadding: 0.4m (15¾in)
Stockinette tubing: 0.4m (15¾in)
Plain fabric in a co-ordinating colour: 0.4m (15¾in)
Matching sewing thread
Medium piping cord: 1.5m (1½yds)

METHOD

1 Check that the needlepoint panel is still square - if there is slight distortion, block back to shape. Make a paper template of the finished needlepoint design. Cut the foam to the shape of the paper template, adding 0.5cm (¼in) all round; this will ensure a snug fit when it is placed in the cushion cover.

2 Wrap with the polyester wadding, cutting away any excess and securing together with a loose herringbone stitch.

3 Cover this pad with the stockinette tubing and sew up the open ends using herringbone stitch (fig. 4).

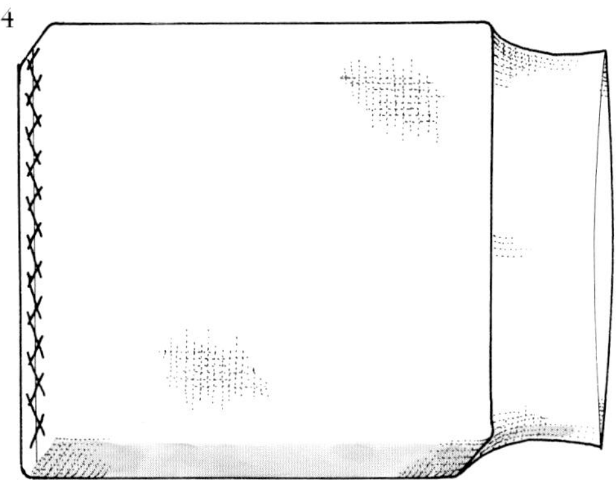

4 Cut the fabric for the back panel to the template size, plus 1.5cm (⅝in) seam allowance on all sides.

5 Make up 1.5m (5ft) of piping in the same fabric, unless a contrast colour is preferred.

6 Attach the piping to the right side of the needlepoint, matching up the seam allowances. Tack together first, then machine stitch, taking care that all unstitched canvas is covered and that the stitching does not encroach on the needlepoint. Join up the piping ends neatly.

8 Place the right sides of the needlepoint and backing fabric together, and machine stitch 1.5cm (5/8 in) from the raw edges, ensuring that the stitching line is very close to the piping. Leave an opening along the back edge of about 27cm (10½in).

5

9 Strip the corners of the seam allowances and neaten the raw edges with a machine zig-zag stitch (fig. 5). Turn right side out. Insert the cushion pad and slip stitch to close the opening.

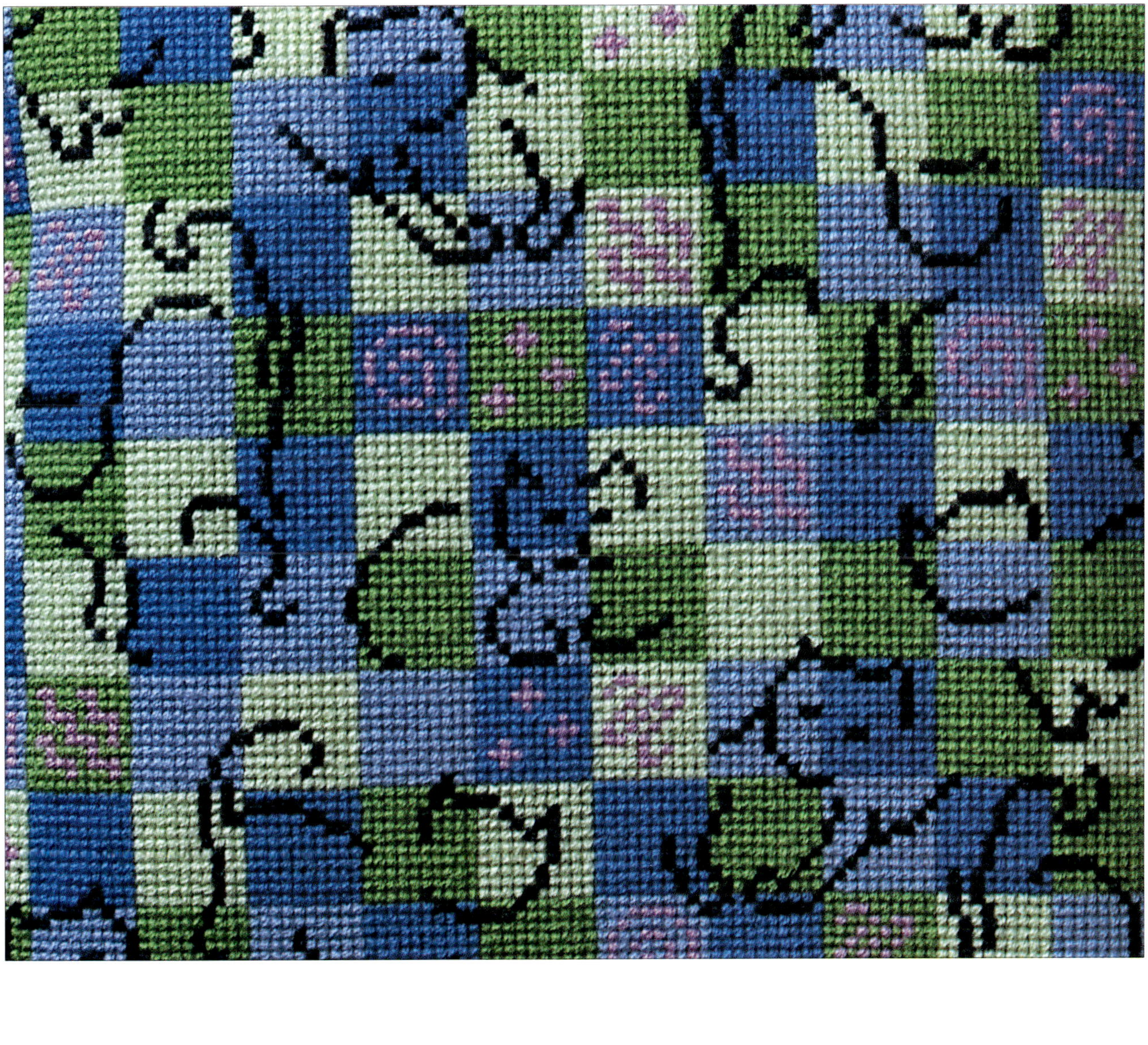

Needlepoint Requirements

The quality of needlepoint for upholstered items is all-important, because it ensures that the piece wears well and looks good over a period of time. There are examples of needlepoint in the Victoria & Albert Museum in London which are between two and three hundred years old; it would be interesting to discover whether any of our present day needlepoint survives so long.

To achieve this necessary and desirable quality, we must look at the different elements that make up a piece of needlepoint.

1. Canvas

The best canvas has a strong mesh of threads so that it wears well, distorts less during stitching and will withstand the rigours of blocking and stretching. An even thickness of warp and weft threads is also essential, as the finished needlepoint will be pulled and strained in all directions when attached to the chair seat. Finally, a canvas mesh should not have any slubs, knots, or irregularities, as these could be natural weak spots.

The three main types of canvas are:

- mono (or single) canvas, with the warp and weft threads woven under and over one another.
- interlock canvas, in which each vertical thread is made up of two thinner threads woven around the thicker horizontal ones.
- double (or Penelope) canvas, which has pairs of interwoven warp and weft threads.

All these types of canvas are suitable for upholstery and it is often worthwhile stitching a small sample of each to decide on a personal preference. There are a few other considerations that should be borne in mind before a final choice is made:

On the basis of feel alone, a favoured canvas is the polished mono de luxe, which is made up of heavier gauge threads. However, for a lightweight piece of furniture with limited space for attaching the needlepoint, this canvas may be too thick and heavy. It is also worth remembering that the threads on mono canvas can sometimes move if the yarn is pulled tightly or if it is very thick.

Interlock canvas can be more difficult than others to block and stretch back into shape. It is therefore not the best canvas for a piece of needlepoint worked entirely in continental tent stitch, or one of the similar decorative stitches.

Double mesh canvas can sometimes be confusing to count if several, different sized stitches are being worked. However, it is useful for petitpoint and tramming.

The colours, mesh sizes and widths available vary for the different types of canvas. Double canvas has a wider range of gauges to choose from but is generally narrower in width than other types, and antique coloured canvas usually has a more limited range of mesh sizes.

As a rough guide when buying canvas, the better the quality, the higher the price and to ensure good quality, it is always advisable to choose a canvas from a reputable manufacturer.

2. Thread

For needlepoint, thread should be strong and hard-wearing, of consistent thickness, have minimum fluff or hair, be colourfast, moth and insect proof, and of a consistent dye. Woollen yarns have been favoured for needlepoint since medieval times, although silk was popular in past centuries as well, much more so than today. Wool is the most hard-wearing of the natural fibres, attracts less dirt because of its lack of static electricity and has a natural resilience, which helps it to keep its appearance.

The main ranges of wools for needlepoint are shown below:

Name	Type	Number of colours
DMC	Tapestry	463
DMC	Broder Médicis	180
(4 strands equivalent to 1 tapestry)		
Appletons	Tapestry	420
Appletons	Crewel	420
(3 strands equivalent to 1 tapestry)		
Anchor	Tapestry	475
Paterna	Persian yarn	417
(easily separated)		
(2 strands equivalent to 1 tapestry)		

Take into account the following considerations: Crewel wool has an advantage in that a varying number of strands can be used for different canvas mesh sizes, and it is fine enough for petitpoint and for tramming threads. It can also be used for subtle shading by mixing strands of varying shades in the needle at the same time.

Personal preference is again a strong element here, as the various wools do stitch slightly differently. Paterna Persian, for example, has a slightly twisted appearance.

Although the number of colours in each range is fairly similar, the emphasis varies from soft, muted colours to bright, vibrant shades. It may be that one range is more suitable for a particular project than another. Colour shade cards are available and these are excellent when making a selection, as the colours can then be viewed in daylight rather than under the artificial light in shops.

Some manufacturers produce hanks for some of the shades in their range. These work out more economical, if you are using a large quantity.

One final word on wools, do try, wherever possible, to buy the complete quantity needed for a project at the same time, as dye lots do sometimes vary a little. Although the difference may be only slight, it is amazing how obvious it can be when stitched, especially on a plain background.

Perlé cotton has been used just once on the padded box, where durability was not a factor.

3. Needles

Good quality tapestry needles should have blunt points so that neither the canvas mesh nor yarn already stitched, is pierced and split. The eyes should be large enough to enable the wool to fit freely and not cause wear as in a tight, small eye space. They should be made with a rust-free finish for smooth stitching. Some are now gold plated, instead of the usual nickel plated steel; these are not only lovely to stitch with, but can be used by people allergic to steel needles.

In order to produce a piece of quality needlepoint, it is important to use the right size needle, not only for the yarn being stitched, but also for the canvas mesh. Too large a needle will push the canvas threads apart, resulting in slightly irregular and distorted stitches.

For the following canvas sizes, use the appropriate size needle as set out below:

3-6 hpi,	needle size 13
7-9 hpi,	needle size 16
10-12 hpi,	needle size 18
13-15 hpi,	needle size 20
16-20 hpi,	needle size 22

4. Coverage of the canvas

The correct coverage of the canvas by the thread used is important, not only for appearance but also because it greatly affects the durability of the needlepoint. Upholstery fabrics, when they are produced, are graded into categories according to their wearing properties. This is measured by means of a 'Martindale Abrasion Test', and the resulting figures are a record of the number of rubs that a fabric can withstand; a good quality fabric has a figure of approximately 60,000. With such an emphasis placed on the resilience of upholstery fabric, bear in mind that it is just as important to achieve the right canvas coverage and tension of stitching if you wish your needlepoint to last and wear well.

If the wool is too thick, the stitches distort the canvas threads, resulting in a bumpy and uneven surface. The wool is also likely to split as the stitches fight for available space. Conversely, if a wool does not cover adequately, gaps of unstitched canvas will be visible. Not only does this look unsightly, but the stitches will be more subject to wear, as they are not part of a continuous surface.

This coverage is also linked to the type of stitch being worked; cross stitch, for example, obviously requires a thinner wool or larger gauge canvas than tent stitch. An ideal combination for upholstery needlepoint is one strand of tapestry wool on a 12hpi canvas, using tent or basketweave stitch. On a 14hpi canvas, whether one strand of tapestry wool or the thinner combination of two strands of crewel wool are used, will depend on the actual wool brand, stitches to be worked and the pattern of the needlepoint. Remember also that, where there are numerous colour changes, starting and finishing creates extra bulk. It is always a good idea to test the wool, canvas and stitch together on a small sample beforehand.

5. Stitches

Needlepoint stitches which cover the back, as well as the front, of the canvas will have harder wearing properties. Continental tent stitch (fig. 1, page 92) and basketweave (fig. 2, page 92) are the obvious ones to use, as both have their wrong sides covered by a dense layer of wool. However neither of these stitches are altogether ideal.

Firstly, tent stitch can distort the canvas even if it is securely attached to a frame, although blocking or stretching can rectify this, if carried out repeatedly. With severe distortion the strength of the canvas may be weakened. Basketweave stitch does not create this problem, as the stitches on the wrong side lie in opposite directions, thus counteracting any pull. Unfortunately, because it is worked in diagonal lines, basketweave is unsuitable for small, irregular shaped areas and randomly positioned lines. However, it is ideal for backgrounds and should be used for these wherever possible. An ideal combination, as can be seen in many of the projects, is to work the pattern and central motifs in continental tent stitch, and the surrounding background in basketweave.

Cross stitch is another suitable stitch as, although the wrong side of the canvas is not fully covered (fig. 3, page 92), the right side is doubly thick. This was a very popular stitch for the Berlin woolwork in Victorian times and is very much favoured by designers today when creating an authentic Victorian look. Initially, cross stitch might seem to take twice the amount of time as other stitches; however, without a frame, you can complete a stitch in two needle movements instead of four (fig. 4, page 92). Again, which you choose to adopt will come down to personal preference.

Half cross stitch is not usually recommended for upholstered items, as it does not cover the wrong side of the canvas and only provides a thin right side coverage. This could be substantially improved by tramming threads. It has, however, been used on the padded box on page 64. It is worked in the same way as method 2 of the cross stitch without completing the crosses. Straight stitch, either random (fig. 5, page 92) or regularly positioned, as in Florentine or Bargello (fig. 6, page 92), will provide a well covered front and back canvas, provided that the

A close-up of the needlepoint for the stool on page 43 demonstrating the fine effect of different decorative stitches

13 Cushion Stitch

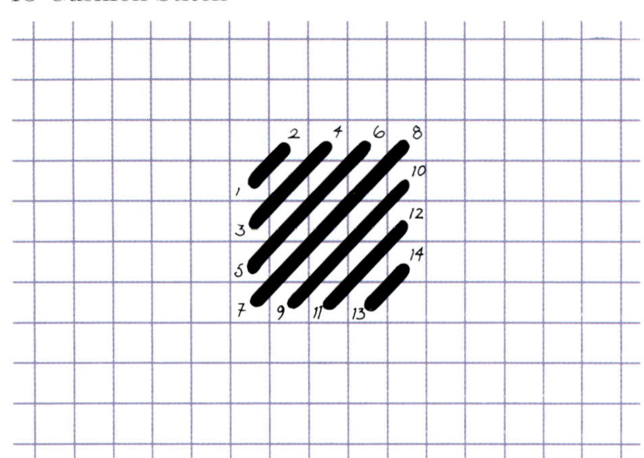

16 Hungarian Diamond

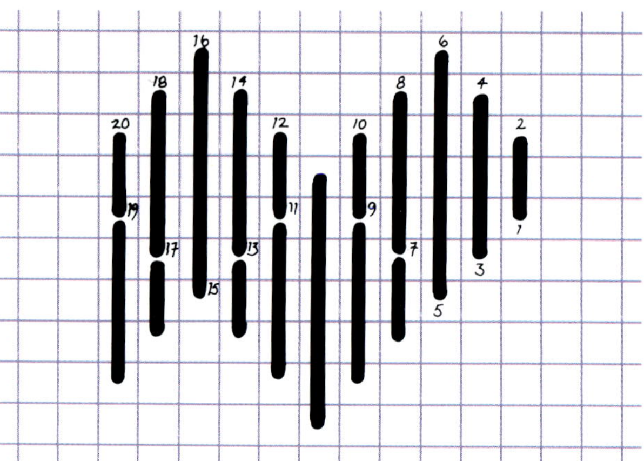

14 Reversed Cushion Stitch

17 Byzantine

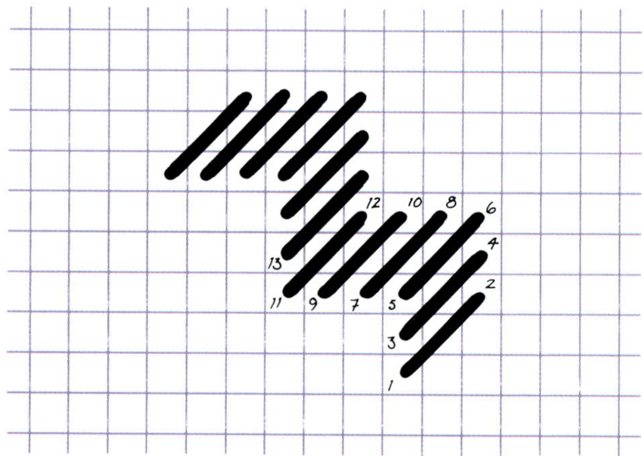

15 Milanese Stitch

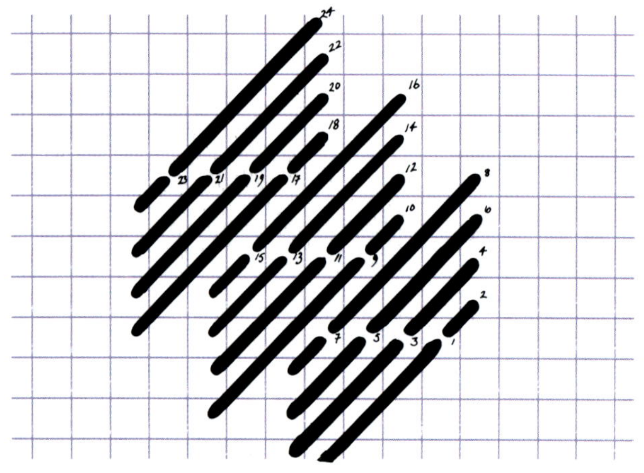

18 Horizontal and Vertical Satin Stitch

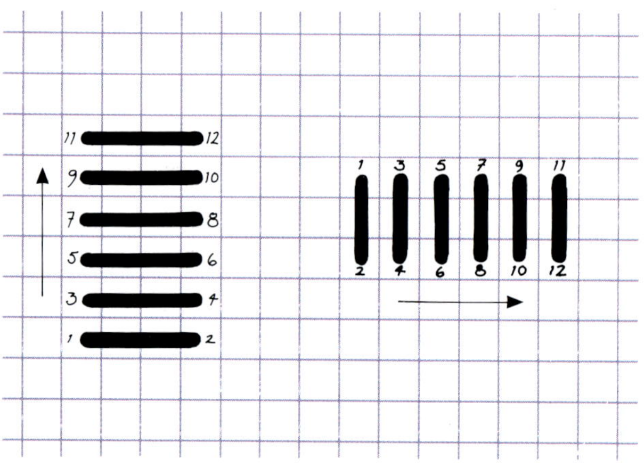

stitches are not excessive in length, as this increases the likelihood of snagging and thus poor wearability.

Diagrams on the previous two pages show several of the wide range of decorative stitches which could provide a suitably durable surface - for example, diagonal mosaic, brick and oblong cross with back stitch (figs. 7, 8 and 9).

Also illustrated are further decorative stitches which have been used or are suggested as alternatives for the sprung stool on page 43 (detail shown on page 91): Byzantine, diagonal scotch, cushion, satin, Florentine and Hungarian diamond stitch. And as an alternative: diagonal mosaic, Milanese and triangle stitch.

A detail of the panel of lilies from the chair on page 59

6. Frames

There are both advantages and disadvantages in using frames for needlepoint. A greatly improved tension is usually achieved with a frame, since the tautness of the canvas ensures the stitching is more consistent. A frame also dramatically decreases any distortion of the canvas, as well as reducing the amount of handling of the canvas and stitching already completed.

There are several different types of frames, including slate, stretcher, roller, and tubular pvc; varying in size from large floor-standing to small hand-held. All should have the canvas attached in both directions to obtain maximum tautness (fig. 19). You may find it necessary to have more than one frame to suit the size of project being stitched.

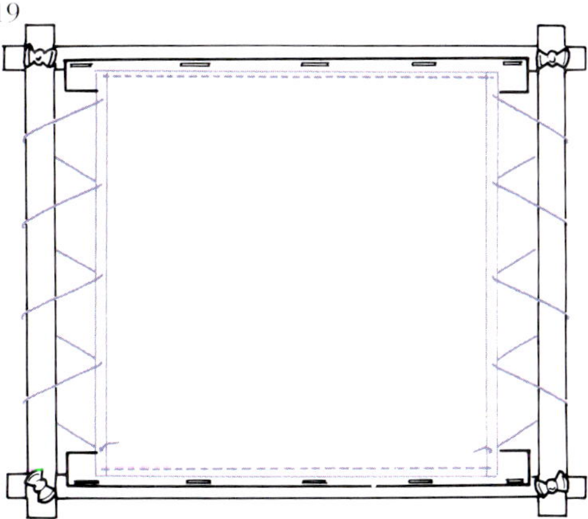

7. Stretching or Blocking

This is a means of re-shaping a stitched canvas back to its original shape and is necessary before the needlepoint can be made up into the finished article. It would be preferable if this process could be avoided, as it stretches and strains the canvas mesh in all directions. The use of a frame will keep the distortion down to a minimum, making the blocking task less laborious.

The technique can be easily carried out at home with very little equipment, although most needlework shops now offer a canvas stretching service, using a purpose-made stretching device. If, at any time, you have the opportunity to use one of these

Upholstery Requirements

Now that all the component parts needed to produce a quality needlepoint have been considered, it is necessary to have a chair or stool seat of the same standard. Once the old top cover is removed, the criteria to look for are:

• There should be a calico covering in good condition, without rips or tears, and with no threadbare areas.

• The calico should look smooth all over and, when pressed, the surface should not reveal any lumps, bumps, dips or hollows.

• Check that the tension of the calico is tight and that, when a hand is run over the seat, no slack or surplus material appears.

• The seat should be of good overall appearance and shape, slightly domed in the centre and even on all sides.

If all these standards are met, then the only upholstery work that would seem to be required is the attaching of the new needlepoint cover. Do not, however, assume that this is the case before removing the old covering material, as it often turns out to be holding the inside of the seat together. Once it is removed, a variety of problems can become evident. Using the list of faults and remedies given with each project should help you to decide how much or how little work needs to be carried out. You will soon notice that the more advanced upholstering of deeper seats utilises and builds on the layers and techniques of the simpler ones. Explanations and instructions for all the necessary techniques are given within this chapter.

Measurements

As measurements of frame sizes vary so much, it will be helpful for you to know where to measure for each layer of material. The following notes describe the main seat types.

Drop-in seat
Webbing and 12oz hessian: 1cm (⅜in) beyond frame.
Linterfelt: measure over the stuffing.
Calico: measure over the linterfelt and stuffing, down the sides and extending 5cm (2in) underneath on all sides.
Polyester wadding: measure over the calico, extending 1cm (⅜in) underneath on all sides.
Needlepoint: measure over the wadding, extending 0.5cm (¼in) underneath frame and adding 5cm (2in) for unstitched canvas on all sides.

Pin-cushion seat
Webbing and 12oz hessian: as for drop-in seat.
Linterfelt: measure over stuffing (approximately 1cm (⅜in) from edge of show-wood).
Calico: measure over the linterfelt and stuffing, extending 5cm (2in) beyond linterfelt on all sides.
Polyester wadding: measure over calico, finishing over the tacks securing the calico.
Needlepoint: measure over the wadding to edges of show-wood, with 5cm (2in) unstitched canvas added on all sides.

Sprung seat without show-wood
Webbing and 12oz hessian: as for drop-in seat.
10oz hessian: measure over stuffing extending 2 cm (¾in) underneath on all sides.
Linterfelt: measure over 2nd stuffing and finishing

on the tacks securing the 10oz hessian.
Calico: measure over linterfelt and stuffing, down the sides and extending 5cm (2in) beyond the frame on all sides.
Polyester wadding and needlepoint: as for drop-in seat.

Non-sprung/sprung seat with show-wood
See page 33.

Tools and materials

Tools for traditional upholstery

- *Hammer* - a small headed one is best. An actual upholsterer's hammer has one magnetic face, which will hold a tack before it is inserted into the seat frame. This facility is very useful when only one hand is free to hammer because the other is holding the fabric in position. It does, however, take a little practice to position the tack exactly.

- *Tack remover* - for taking out tacks which are not flush with the frame, that is, not 'hammered home'. It is essential for removing 'temporary tacks', that is, those placed only halfway in to hold the material in a position that may well be altered more than once. The 'claw' of the tack remover may be part of a hammer head, making it unnecessary to have it as a separate tool.

- *Wooden mallet and ripping chisel* - for removing old tacks or those fully hammered in. If a hammer is used instead of a mallet, the chisel handle will soon become damaged.

- *Webbing stretcher* - various types are available, all of which hold the webbing taut while the tacks are hammered in position. Overstretching will result in the webbing disintegrating around the tacks, or damage to the seat frame. Pulling the webbing by hand does not create a sufficiently strong tension, so that it will sag from the start.

- *Mattress needle* - this is a double pointed needle used for stitching 'stuffing ties' and for building up stitched edges around the seat. Various lengths are available, a 25cm (10in) being an average size.

- *Curved or semi-circular needle* - for sewing bridle loops and attaching the springs; a medium size of 12.5cm (5in) is probably the most useful.

- *Small curved needle* - for ladder stitching and attaching trimmings; a fine 3.75cm(1½in) is best.

- *Regulator* - for regulating or moving the stuffing before stitching the firm edges and roll.

Tools for modern upholstery

- *Staple gun* - many different types are available, including electric ones. Select a staple gun suitable for the tasks in hand - for example, the lighter weight one may have insufficient power to drive a staple fully into a piece of wood, especially hardwood. It should also be able to take a variety of staple sizes 6-13mm (¼ - ⅝in) in length.

- *Staple remover* - makes the taking out of any staples easier than improvising with other tools.

Materials

Webbing: black, or brown and white herringbone weave webbing is recommended for all seats, as it is stronger than the cheaper jute ones.

Springs: traditional coil or hour glass springs vary both in size (height) and gauge (strength of the steel wire). It is important to make the correct decision on both of these measurements when replacing springs. The height of the selected springs should be roughly equal to the finished height of the seat, as the subsequent layers of stuffing and padding make up the space when the springs are compressed, that is, about 2.5cm (1in). The gauge for a seat should be fairly hard - a nine gauge, for example - whereas the backs and arms of a chair would require a softer gauge of ten or twelve.

Hessian: a12oz weight of hessian is used to cover the webbing and springs, as its close weave will not only wear well, but also prevent strands of stuffing from penetrating through. A 10oz hessian has a looser weave which makes it lighter weight and is used where stitching of the side edges of a seat is required. Scrim can be used instead of

10oz hessian; it is made of linen and is a much finer weave, but is a lot more expensive.

Stuffing: suitable loose stuffings are either vegetable fibre or animal hair. The latter is softer and more expensive, but is easier to work with and usually produces a better result. For seats with two layers of stuffing, economise by using fibre for the underneath first stuffing, and hair for the thinner, second stuffing. Rubberised hair, that is hair held together by latex spray, can be bought in sheets, either 2.5cm (1in) or 5cm (2in) in thickness. This makes the stuffing process very much quicker and less messy; however, it has the major disadvantage of restricted use because of its uniform thickness. Old horsehair taken out of a seat can be re-used, either by re-teasing or washing it. Upholsterers may have a carding machine and be willing to put the hair through this for a small charge. If the hair is to be washed, either hand wash in a bath or, for machine washing, first place into two pillowcases, tied securely or stitched closed. When dry, the hair can be re-teased and re-used. Fibre, on the other hand, is not really suitable for re-cycling, unless very new, as it becomes brittle with age and breaks up.

Foam: latex foam, made from rubber, and synthetic polyurethane, made from chemicals, are both available in various densities and thicknesses. All foam now has to be flame retardant to comply with the relatively recent 'Fire Regulations for Furniture and Furnishings 1988'.

Linterfelt and Skin Wadding: both are made from cotton fibres; linterfelt is about 1.25cm (½in) thick and skin wadding about 0.3-0.6cm (⅛-¼in) thick. These are barrier materials to prevent the stuffing from working through into the calico and covering fabric.

Polyester Wadding: a synthetic wadding used between the calico and top covering fabric for extra padding. It covers any slight irregularities in the calico shape, producing a better looking overall finish. For traditionalists, skin wadding can be used instead.

Calico: a strong cotton fabric used to contain the padding and stuffing beneath. It is attached under tension so as to provide a firm base over which to place the covering needlepoint. Both flame-retardant and non-flame-retardant calico are available: the former feels stiffer and less user-friendly. According to the current Fire Regulations, furniture made after 1950 must use all flame-retardant fillings and materials.

Bottoming: black calico is used to cover the underneath of a seat. Hessian can be used as an alternative material and is found in many older chairs, while a flame-retardant, non-woven black material made of polypropylene is now used for modern furniture. Bottoming is not necessary where all the upholstery is attached to the top or sides of a frame or seat, as for a pin-cushion, top stuffed piece.

Tacks: sizes to use:
for lacing springs - 16mm (⅝in) improved
for webbing, 12oz and 10oz hessian - 13mm (½in) improved
for needlepoint, calico - 10mm (⅜in) fine
'Improved' tacks have both larger heads and thicker shanks than fine ones. The size denotes the length of the shank.

Gimp Pins: these are small-headed coloured tacks with 13mm (½in) long, thin shanks, used for attaching trimmings.

Staples: average sized staples are 13-10mm (½-⅜in) in length.

Twine: upholsterer's twine is waxed mattress twine and is available in various thicknesses. Choose a medium size which can be used for all purposes - for example, no. 2.

Laid Cord: a thick cord, made of jute, used for lacing the springs together.

The two main types of upholstery, traditional and modern, have both been used for the projects. These differ not only in the materials used to make the seat, but also in the techniques employed and tools required. Finished pieces may, in fact, look quite similar, but will certainly feel different. Traditional upholstery is firm and solid, whereas the foam in modern upholstery is softer and has greater springiness. The nature of foam means that, in ten years time, it will have become compressed and will need replacing, whereas the traditional seat will only be in its infancy, with many more years to go.

Layers and Techniques

1. WEBBING

The strips, as a general rule, should be placed about one webbing width apart, as a greater distance will not provide sufficient support. Whenever possible, position a strip in the centre of the seat rather than on either side of it; however, this does depend on the overall dimensions of the frame. Unless a seat is sprung, the webs are always attached to the top side of the seat frame.

Instructions

• Mark the centre of each side of the frame with chalk, then place the first piece of webbing over the centre back, folding over 2cm (½ -¾in). Position the fold three quarters of the way towards the back of the tacking rail. Hammer five 13mm (½in) tacks as shown, hammering each all the way in (fig. 1).

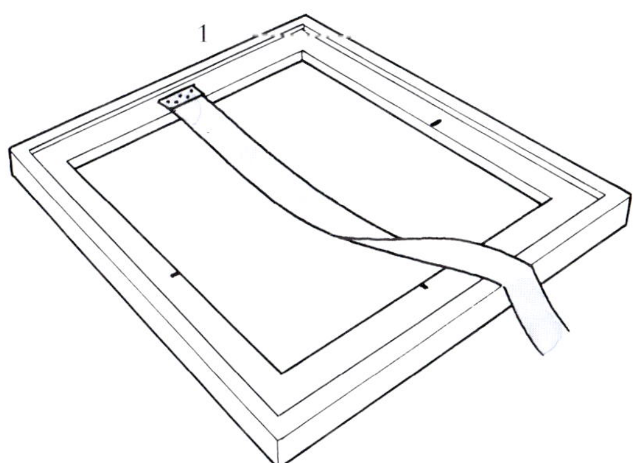

• Using the webbing stretcher, pull the end of the webbing tightly, so that it feels 'twangy' when fingers drum on it. Hammer in three tacks as shown (fig. 2).

• Cut the webbing 2cm (½-¾in) from the tacks, fold over and hammer in two more tacks in between (fig. 3).

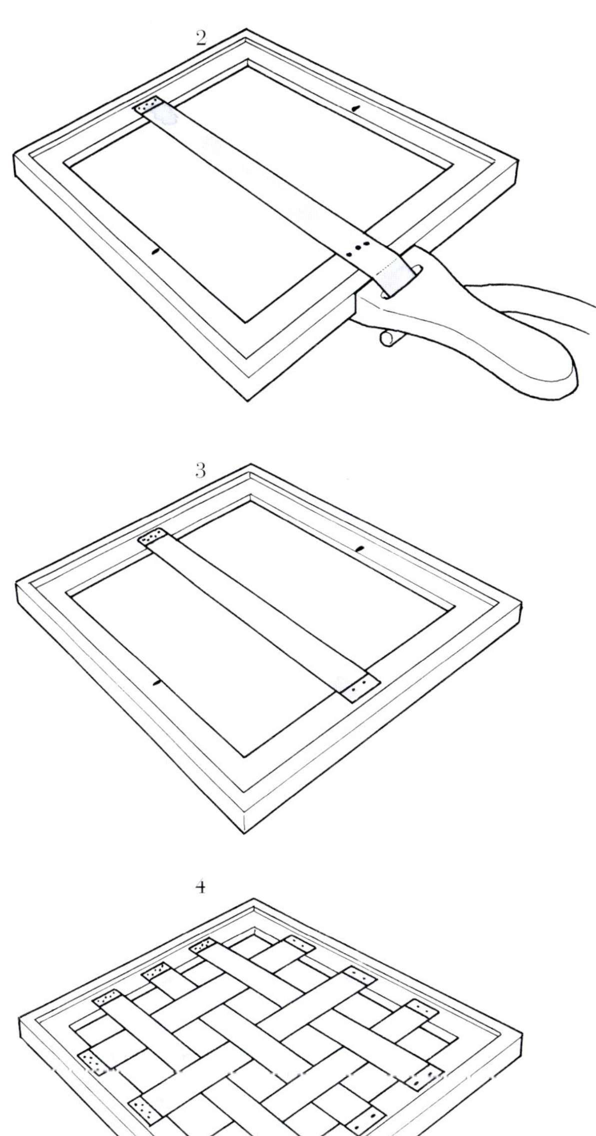

• Repeat the process with each vertical webbing strip.

• Attach the webs horizontally this time, lining up the centre mark and interweaving them with the vertical ones (fig. 4).

2. SPRINGS

These should be placed about 2.5cm (1in) away from the frame edge and be at least this distance apart from each other. The total number required depends on the frame size : a large square stool would probably have five with one in the centre, as would a dining chair seat, unless very small, in which case three would be sufficient (fig. 5).

5

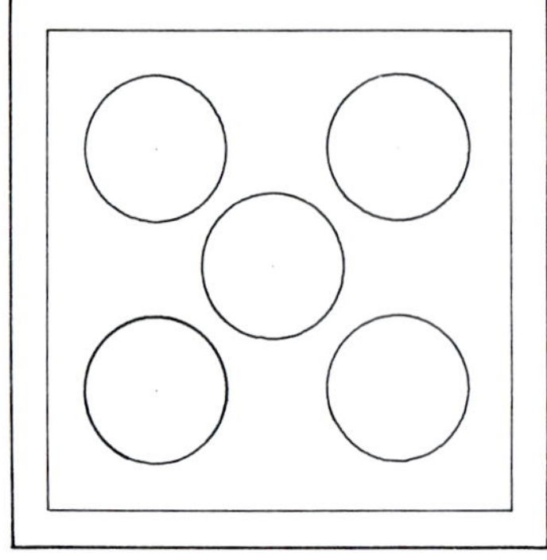

Instructions

A. Attaching to the webbing

• Place the springs on the webbing base, with the upper knot facing towards the centre and the bottom knot lying on the webbing strip. Draw round each spring with chalk.

• Remove the springs except for one at the back; sew one at a time from underneath the webbing, using a length of twine and a curved needle (fig. 6a), starting with an upholsterer's knot (fig. 22, page 105).

6a

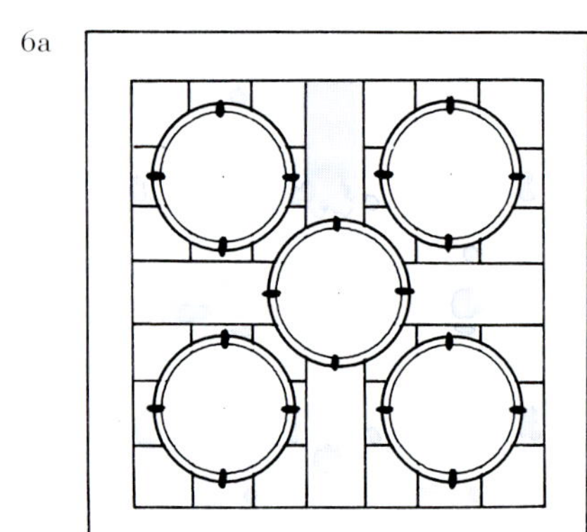

6b

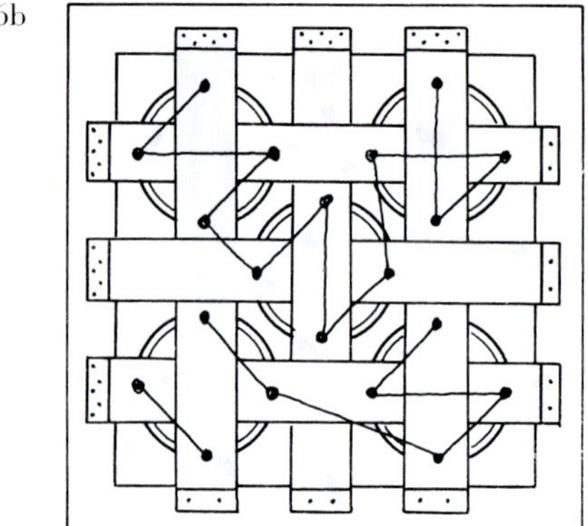

7

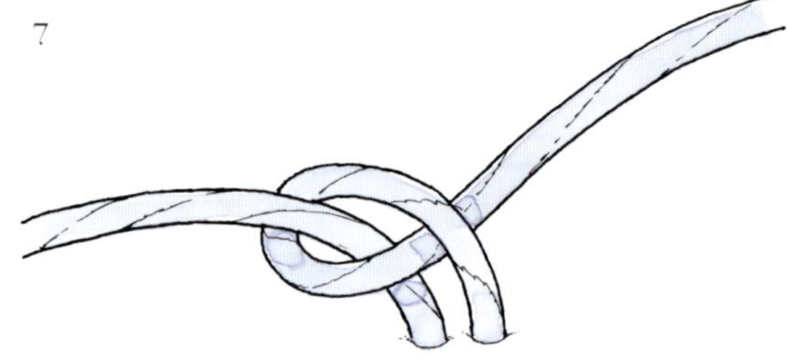

8

• Secure the spring to the webbing in three or four places (fig. 6b) with half-hitch knots (fig. 7). Move on to the next spring until all are attached.

• Finish off the twine with several clove-hitch knots (fig. 8).

B. Lacing the springs

• Temporary tack two 16mm (⅝in) improved tacks into the topside of the seat frame, 0.5cm (⅛in) apart, opposite the centre of each spring (fig. 9).

• Cut a length of laid cord for each row of springs. Measure this by laying the cord over the row and doubling the length.

9

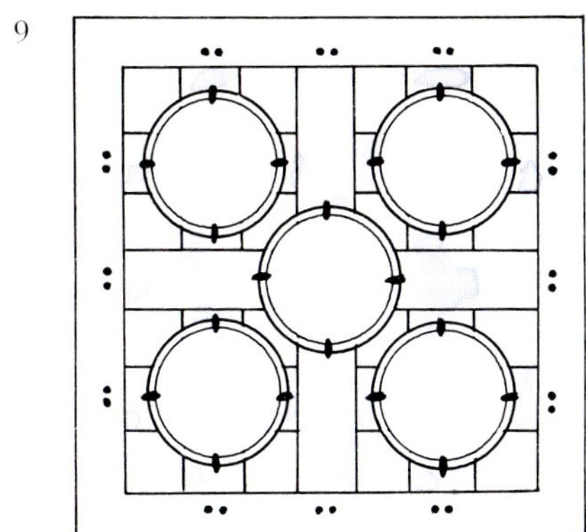

10

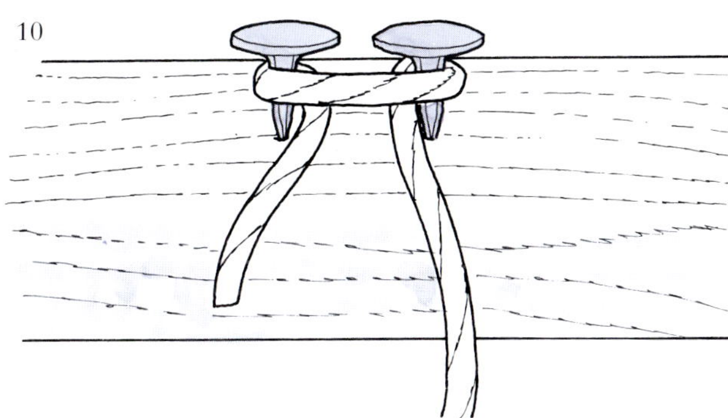

• Working from back to front, attach one end of the cord to the tacks (fig. 10), then to the top coil of the first spring with a hitch knot (fig. 11). Hammer the tacks fully home once the cord is attached.

11

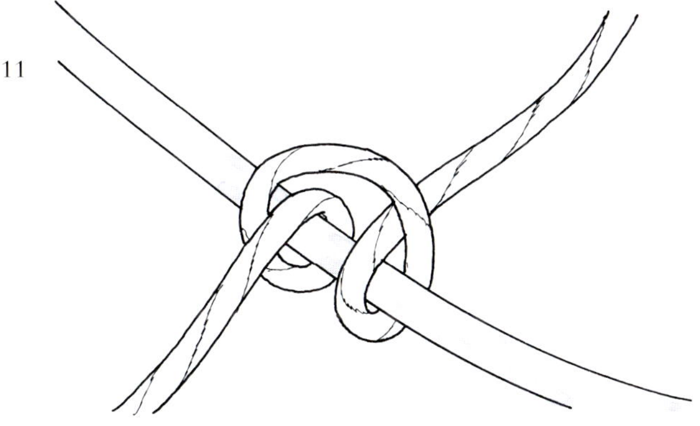

• The knots attaching the cord to the springs always start and finish with a hitch knot and alternate in between with half-hitches (fig. 12). When these knots are being made, the springs must be compressed by approximately 2.5cm (1in) to the required height.

12

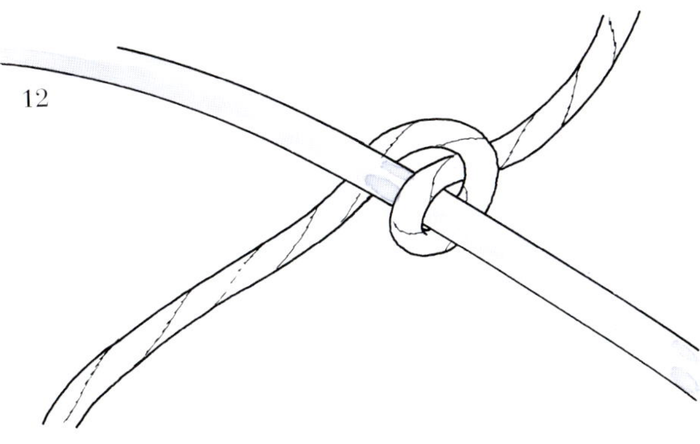

• At the end of the row of springs, secure the laid cord around the two 16mm (⅝in) tacks (fig. 13).

13

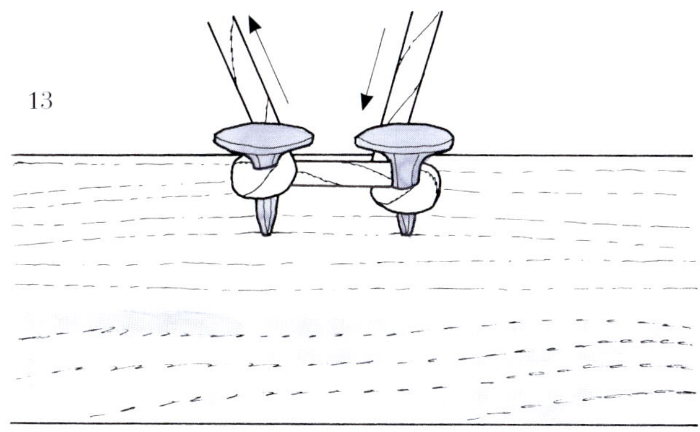

• Repeat for each row, vertically first, then horizontally: fig. 14 shows the result.

14

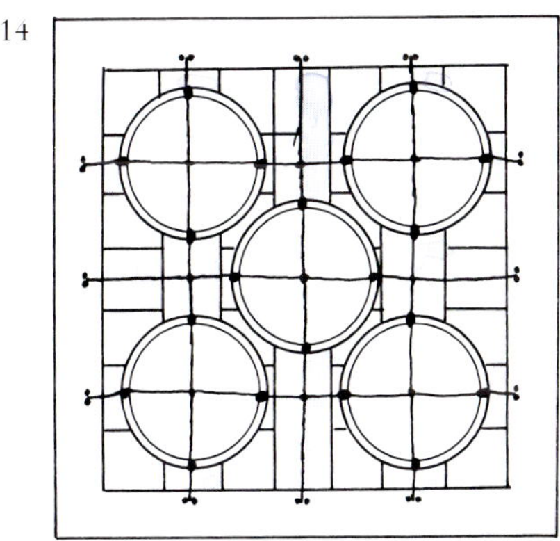

• One slight variation should be made if much larger springs are used: the cord is attached to the second spring coil, instead of to the top of the springs nearest to the frame. This prevents the springs from being pulled over at too sharp an angle, which would eventually result in buckling.

C. Attaching the springs to the 12oz hessian
• Once the hessian is tacked into position, the springs are stitched to it in three or four places, in exactly the same way as they were attached to the webbing (fig. 15). The springs are now firmly secured which means that, when sat upon, they will depress in unison in a vertical direction and give many years of service.

15

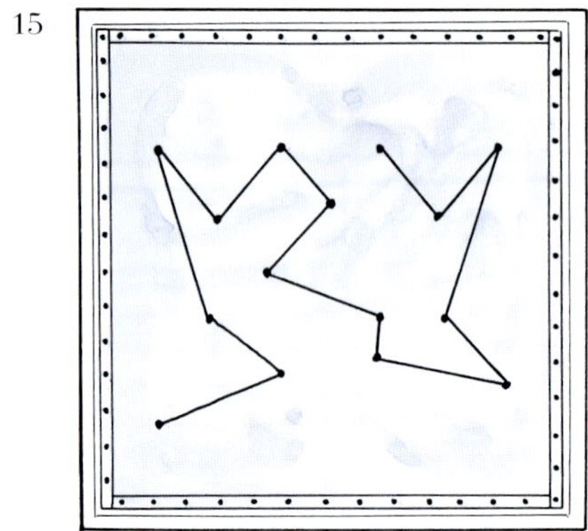

16

17

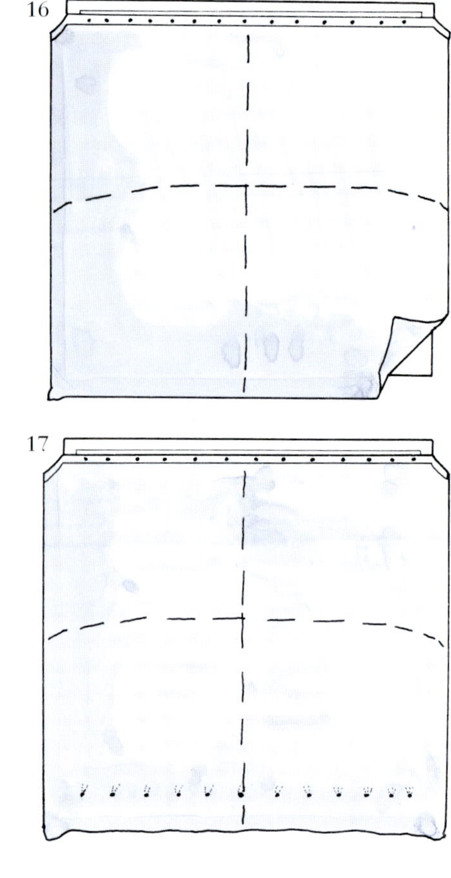

12OZ HESSIAN

This is attached either over the webbing onto the top side of the frame on a non-sprung seat, or over the springs to the same position on the frame.

Instructions
• Mark the centres of each side of the hessian and place on the chair seat, matching up the centre back marks. Fold over 1.5cm (½in) along the back edge of the hessian and hammer home through this double layer, positioning the fold 0.6cm (¼in) away from the show-wood edge and spacing 13mm (½in) fine tacks 2.5cm (1in) apart (fig. 16).

• Pull the hessian tightly towards the front edge and temporary tack, firstly in the centre, then left and right, through a single layer, keeping the grain vertical (fig. 17).

18

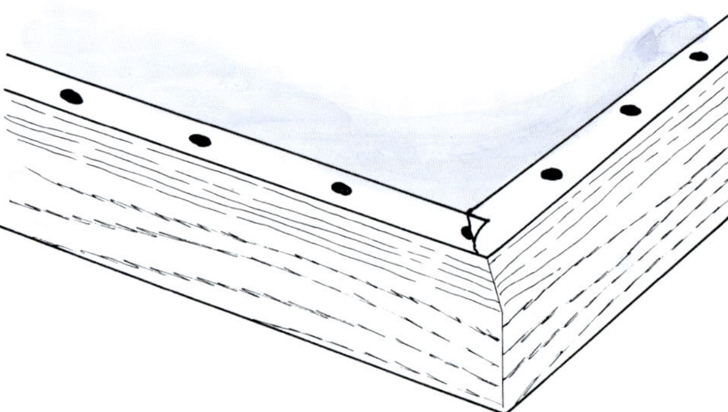

• Now temporary tack along both sides, again 2.5cm (1in) apart and matching up the centre marks.

• Check the hessian is of an even, firm tension all over, then tack home. Fold back the raw edges on the three sides and tack them home (fig. 18), placing tacks 5cm (2in) apart.

4. BRIDLE LOOPS

These are made of twine and hold the loose stuffing in place. The height of the loop, or slack of the twine, varies according to the depth of the stuffing required. It is easier to use your hand and fingers for measuring the loops, rather than a tape measure - for example, flat fingers (fig. 19), and two fingers upright (fig. 20).

Instructions

• Use a curved needle and a length of twine and start with an upholsterer's knot (fig. 21).

• Form the loops with a back stitch. The loops should be about 8-10cm (3-4in) in length, 5cm (2in) away from the edges of the hessian.

• Place the rows of loops about 10cm (4in) apart; the number of rows will depend on the overall size of the seat (fig. 22). Finish with a double knot.

19

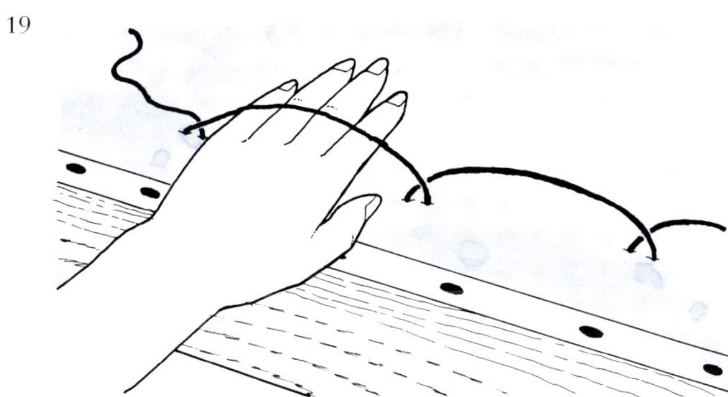

21

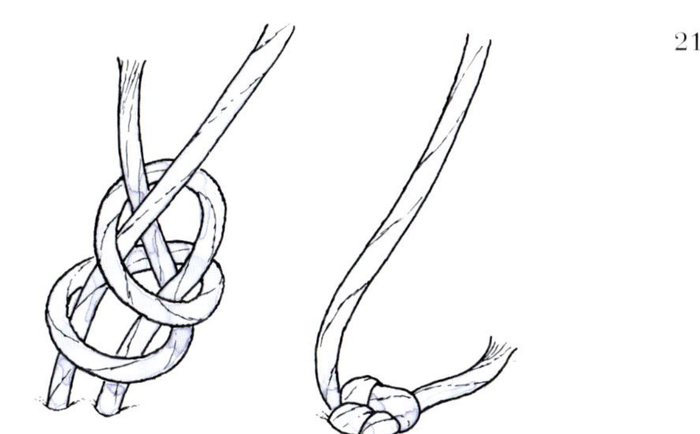

20

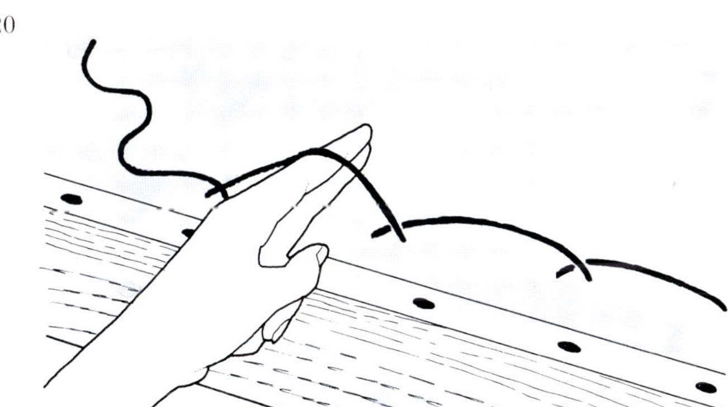

22

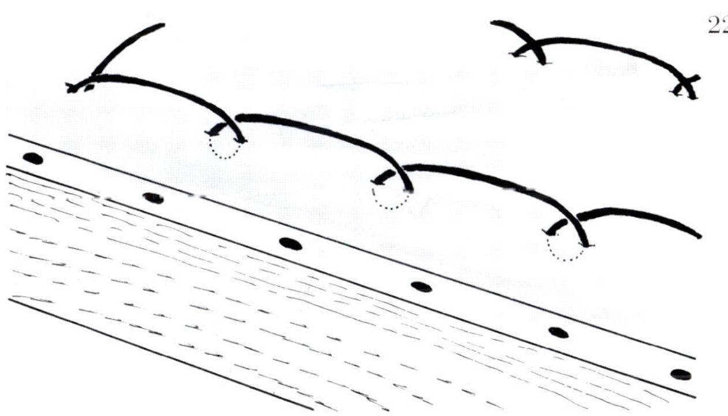

5. STUFFING

Ensure that, whatever stuffing is being used, it is well teased and free of any knots or debris. Be systematic in placing the same size handful under each loop. If more than one seat of the same size is being stuffed, then weigh the stuffing before you start, so that the exact amount can be used for each.

Instructions

• Place a handful under each loop, continuing around a second time until the space under the loops is filled.

• Pull over the stuffing if small gaps are visible between the handfuls, so that an even depth of stuffing is achieved. It is a good idea to close your eyes and just use your hand to feel if the láyer is even, and that all dips and hollows are filled.

• Place a small amount of extra stuffing in the central area to achieve a slightly rounded, domed shape. If the seat is to have stitched sides, place a greater depth of stuffing around the edges of the seat (fig. 23). Pack it firmly, so that there is sufficient quantity to be successfully stitched. The seat will then need a layer of 10oz hessian, stuffing ties, stitched and roll edges, and a second layer of stuffing.

23

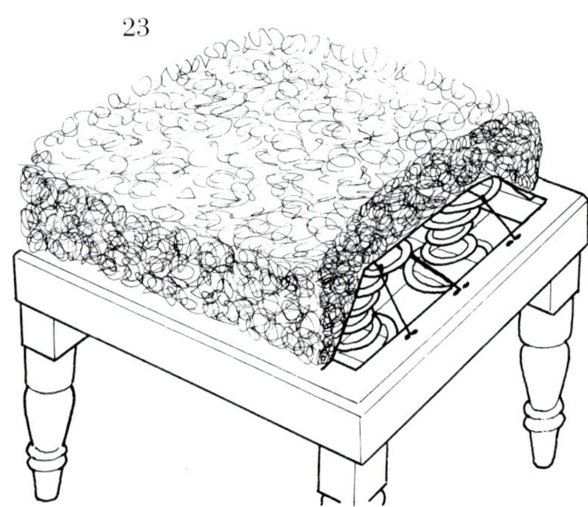

6. 10OZ HESSIAN

This must be cut large enough so that it will cover the stuffing loosely and can be folded around the edges (fig. 24).

24

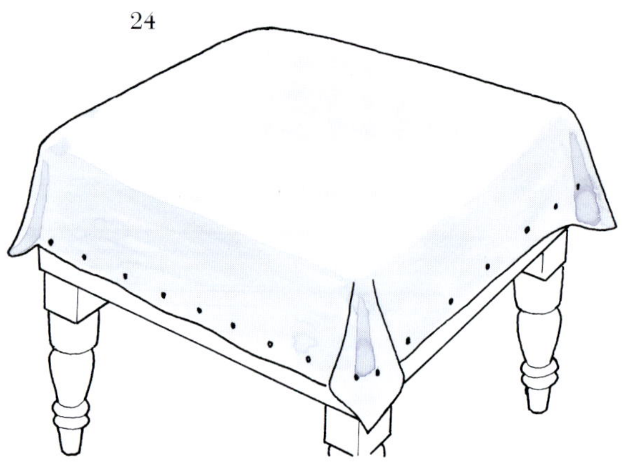

Instructions

• Place over the stuffing and temporary tack, first in the centre, then along each side, so that the hessian is 'hand-tight'.

A. Stuffing ties

• Using a mattress needle and twine, insert stuffing ties through the hessian, stuffing and 10oz hessian only. They are made with a running stitch and should be about 10-13cm (4-5in) long with 1cm (½in) gaps between and are used to hold the stuffing in place, as well the 10oz hessian while it is being attached. Keeping about 10cm (4in) away from the seat edges, stitch the ties in a zig-zag shape (fig. 25). Start with an upholsterer's knot and finish with several half-hitches, after pulling the ties tightly.

25

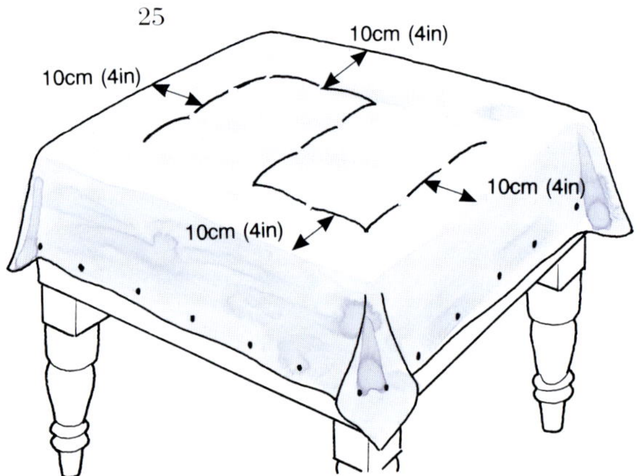

• Remove the temporary tacks, fold the hessian under the stuffing and temporary tack again, this time on the chamfered edge (fig. 26). If there is no chamfer, use a rasp file or plane to make one, as

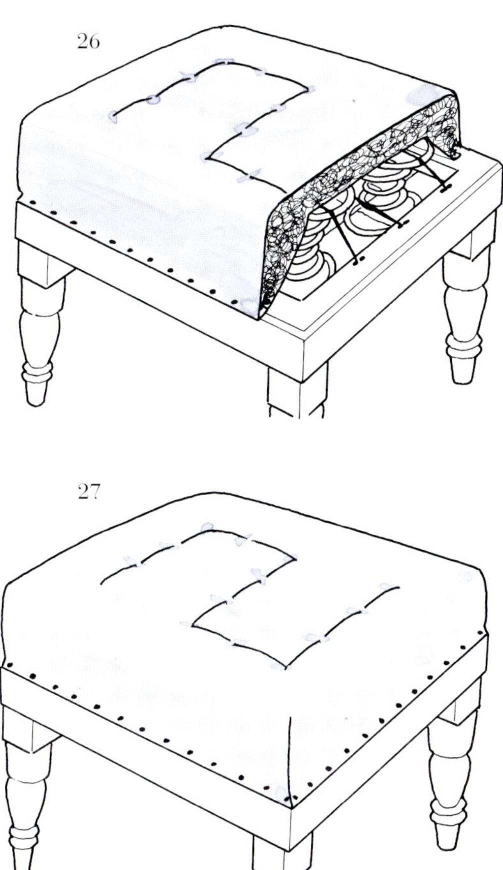

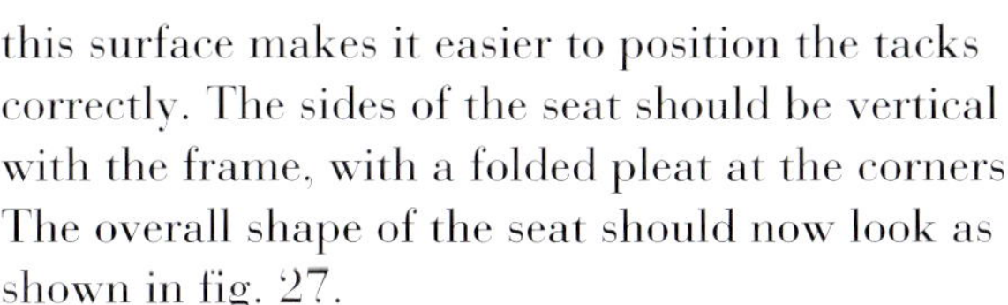

this surface makes it easier to position the tacks correctly. The sides of the seat should be vertical with the frame, with a folded pleat at the corners. The overall shape of the seat should now look as shown in fig. 27.

B. Making a stitched edge

• Tack home all the way around the seat; it is now ready to be stitched. The stitching creates a hard edge above the frame so that, when the seat is sat

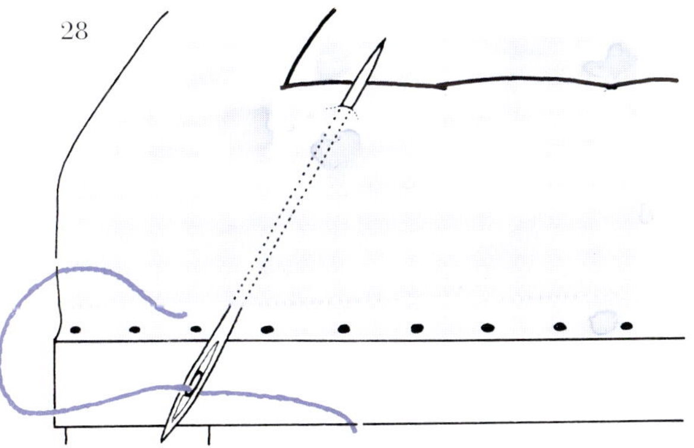

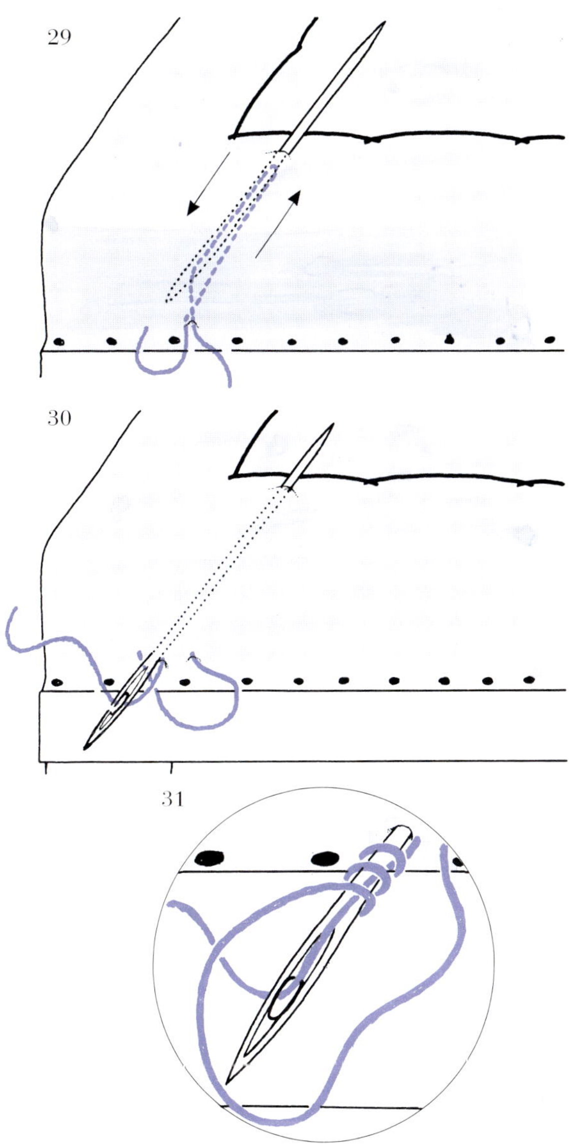

on, it will retain its shape. Use a regulator to push the stuffing towards the edges. For the stitching, use a mattress needle and a long length of twine. Start with an upholsterer's knot, positioning the first row above the line of tack heads. Insert the needle, 2.5cm (1in) from the knot, at an angle, so that the end emerges on the near side of the stuffing ties (fig. 28). Pull through nearly all the way (fig. 29), twist a little, then push the needle back to re-emerge along the line of tack heads, almost at the knot (fig. 30). Leave the needle so that half its length is showing at the front, then wind the twine round three times in an anti-clockwise direction (fig. 31). Take the needle out and pull the twine very tightly. This stitch has pulled and secured the

32

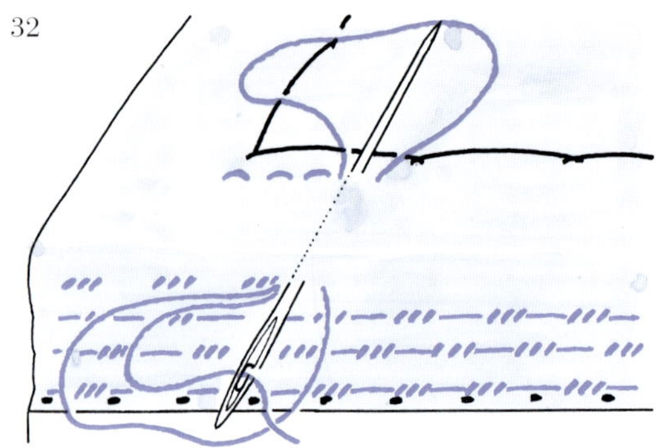

stuffing near the front of the seat edge. Repeat all the way around the seat.

Carry on with rows of blind stitching, spaced about 1cm (½in) apart, remembering to regulate before each row. The number of rows necessary depends on the height of the hessian and stuffing. A 2.5cm (1in) space should be left at the top for a stitched roll to be made; this will give a definite line and shape to the seat, as well as reinforcing the top of the seat edges.

C. Making a roll edge
The method is similar to blindstitching, but this time take the needle right out and make a back stitch (fig. 32). Bring the needle out almost at the starting position and wind the twine around as before.

D. Second layer of stuffing
• Finally, a new set of bridle loops must be stitched to hold the thinner second layer of stuffing. Make the loops flat against the hessian, starting about 5cm (2in) from the stitched edge. Insert a small amount of stuffing covering the entire surface. Check that, when your hand is placed over this, the roll edge cannot be felt through the stuffing, as this would cause discomfort to the sitter.

7. LINTERFELT/SKIN WADDING AND CALICO

• Place over the linterfelt or skin wadding and trim away any excess. The exact positions for finishing this layer can be seen on the individual seat profiles for the projects.

33

34

• Lay over the calico and place one 10mm (⅜in) fine tack temporarily on each side.

• Temporary tack along the back edge, then repeat along the front edge.

• Slowly pull the calico tight by re-tacking the back, then the front; at the same time pull the calico sideways from the centre back and centre front.

• Temporary tack along each side, then keep re-tacking all round until all the slack tension has gone, and the calico is smooth and taut. It is only at this stage that the seat can be felt to see if there are any lumps or hollows. These can be rectified by lifting up the appropriate section of calico and wadding so that you can re-distribute the stuffing.

• The corners on a pin-cushion seat should taper away to nothing, so pleats are unnecessary. On the drop-in seats, two small pleats will be needed either side of the corner (fig. 33). On the top stuffed and sprung seat, fold the corner fabric as shown (fig. 34). Pull the calico tightly on all the corners, so that it is both smooth and taut.

8. NEEDLEPOINT

Measurements to determine the exact size of the needlepoint required for a seat should only be made once the calico layer is in place. This will ensure that neither too little nor too much canvas stitching is worked. For seats where the cover has to negotiate around back frame struts, or substantial pleats are required at the front, the position of these should be marked on the canvas (fig. 35). Non-stitching of such areas has two advantages: not only the obvious one of wasted time and wool but more importantly, when cuts are made, these will be in unstitched canvas, leaving the stitching intact. The disadvantage, however, is that measurements and positioning have to be one hundred percent correct.

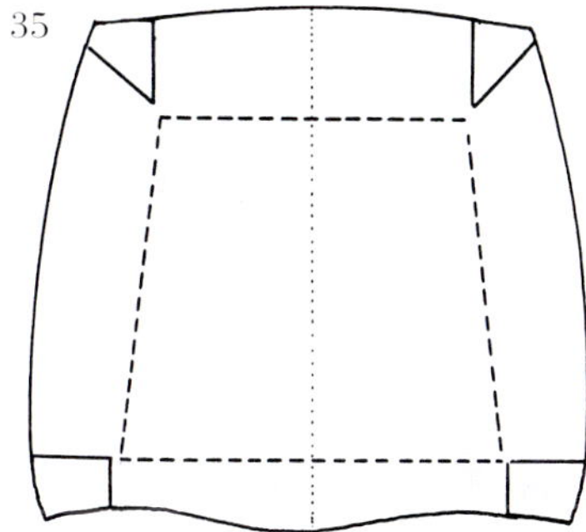
35

Fold under at least 2.5cm (1in) of unstitched canvas when attaching a finished piece of needlepoint to a seat, rather than trimming very closely as for ordinary upholstery fabric. The main advantage of this is that if, for any reason, the cover is removed, then sufficient canvas for handling is still available for re-attaching. If, as a last resort, stitched needlepoint has to be cut, place a layer of clear glue around the area, leave to dry, then carefully cut through the middle. This will prevent any stitches from fraying and becoming unravelled.

9. TRIMMINGS

In upholstery, trimmings are often required to cover raw edges of fabric and tacks or staples. This is usually the case where show-wood occurs on a frame - for example, the Louis XV-Style Dining Chair on page 35. Many commercial trimmings are available, from the plainer narrow braids to the more sumptuous elaborate fringes and tassels. However, for upholstered needlepoint, a non-shiny trimming of a similar texture can often look more appropriate. There are woollen trimmings available but, as an alternative, you can knot your own using the popular friendship bracelet technique, knitted, macrame or plaited as shown on page 23. If the wools from the needlepoint are used, then there will be total colour co-ordination with the seat.

Attach the trimming by slipstitching (fig. 4, page 42) or glueing to the canvas. Anchor the ends of the braid with gimp pins.

10. BOTTOMING

This is used to tidy the underneath of a seat. It is cut 0.5cm (¼in) wider on all sides than the base. To attach, fold under 1.5cm (½in) and tack or staple to the underneath (depending on whether the upholstery method is traditional or modern).

Shade Conversions

Please note that exact equivalents are not available. When selecting colours for a particular design, put the chosen skeins together to ensure the shades are well balanced. There are three lists for the tapestry wools, the first column being the numbers used for the needlepoint in the book.

TAPESTRY WOOL

Anchor	DMC	Appletons
8006	écru	882
8052	7905	841
8058	7727	473
8060	7846	474
8062	7781	696
8294	7191	706
8322	7164	708
8326	7166	223
8330	7169	126
8344	7192	753
8346	7194	222
8352	7199	226
8402	7147	757
8786	7799	742
8788	7283	743
8792	7306	566
8832	7302	322
8834	7592	565
8838	7339	327
8904	7925	328
9002	7369	401
9020	7320	402
9022	7428	406
9252	7400	873
9442	7917	701

Appletons	DMC	Anchor
105	7243	8594
251A	7549	9194
252	7548	9196
253	7547	9198
254	7364	9202
255	7367	9204
322	7294	8832
431	7954	8984
462	7313	8776
465	7247	8612
472	7506	8136
473	7505	8138
474	7437	8140
477	7446	9538
524	7399	8916
525	7598	8918
526	7861	8920
766	7459	9494
821	7316	8688
823	7317	8690
843	7725	8022
864	7920	8238
866	7184	8240
872	7905	8012
884	7709	8584
904	7496	9406
943	7202	8396
944	7204	8416
945	7136	8438
948	7137	8442
992	7453	8006
996	7431	8112

DMC	Appletons	Anchor
7078	471	8038
7115	148	8426
7141	761	9362
7144	861	9444
7147	147	8402
7166	206	8326
7175	862	8324
7176	863	9558
7179	708	9506
7193	222	8364
7194	223	8366
7196	224	8400
7200	751	8342
7275	964	9776
7297	327	8740
7351	251A	9192
7364	255	9202
7398	296	9082
7422	331	9094
7452	701	9382
7453	851	9324
7460	703	9632
7472	472	8038
7503	471	8054
7520	988	9654
7579	692	8052
7583	252	9196
7593	323	8738
7758	225	8400
7950	203	9596
7951	222	8348
écru	992	9502
7308	749	8744

CREWEL WOOL

Use 3 skeins of Appletons instead of 4 DMC

DMC *broder médicis*	Appletons
8100	227
8104	479
8106	226
8107	223
8110	716
8111	707
8113	753
8119	142
8122	714
8123	148
8126	504
8127	503
8128	865
8129	623
8139	621
8164	203
8166	204
8168	206
8173	861
8175	862
8176	863
8208	322
8314	693
8328	872
8341	254
8401	255
8402	256
8410	327
8411	344
8417	547
8419	543
8420	251A
8506	924
8567	421
8896	451
8904	425
8995	483
8996	482
8997	481
navy	749

PERLE COTTON

DMC	Anchor
351	10
352	9
353	6
356	5975
502	877
504	875
518	169
597	168
598	167
676	891
746	386
758	868
931	921
932	343
945	881
948	778
955	206
écru	387

Index

LIST OF SUPPLIERS

Appleton Bros Ltd, Thames Works, Church Street, London W4 2PE

Coats Patons Crafts UK, P O Box 22, The Lingfield Estate, McMullen Road, Darlington, Co Durham D4 1YQ

Colinette Yarns Ltd, The Old Baptist Chapel, Watergate Street, Llanfair Caereinian, Powys, Mid Wales SY21 0RB

DMC Creative World Ltd, Pullman Road, Wigston, Leicestershire LE18 2DY

MacGregor Designs, P O Box 129, Burton upon Trent

ACKNOWLEDGEMENTS

The author would like to thank the following people and companies for supplying materials and furniture and for help with stitching and upholstering the chairs and stools:
Coats Patons Crafts for supplying wool and canvases, as well as stitching two projects; with thanks to Stephanie Baker especially
DMC for supplying tapestry wool, crewel wool and perlé cotton and all Zweigart canvases; with thanks to Cara Ackerman especially
MacGregor Designs for the wooden footstool on page 47
Ann Phillips, Vivien Staunton and Linda Williams for help with the stitching
Pam Brown, Annie Channing-Williams, Rose Cramsie, Jo Richardson and Angela Secker for help with the upholstering
My family for their enthusiastic support